# LIGHTWORKER TRAINING

## A Practical Guide to
## Healing with Energy + Consciousness

Tatiana Sakurai

# TABLE OF CONTENTS

**PART 1 :: CONCEPTS + CONSCIOUSNESS TOOLS**

**CHAPTER 1 : INITIATION**

**CHAPTER 2 : FOUNDATIONS OF HEALING**

## CHAPTER 3: MINDSET AWARENESS

## CHAPTER 4: DEVELOPMENT OF INTUITION

## PART 2 :: MULTIMODALITY ENERGY WORK TECHNIQUES

## CHAPTER 5: INVOCATION + CO-CREATION

## CHAPTER 6: SCANNING ENERGIES + CORD CUTTING

## CHAPTER 7: ENERGY HYGIENE + BIOFIELD CLEARING

## CHAPTER 8: CHAKRA FORM + FUNCTION + CLEARING

## CHAPTER 9: ENERGIZING + SEALING + HARMONIZING

# FOREWORD

I first met Tatiana on a rainy winter day at a seaside lodge in Washington. My heart was broken in a thousand pieces by a disinterested lover. I had no idea how to mend that heart; whether to keep smashing it, numb it with whiskey, or throw it in the ocean. I was in my mid-thirties and still didn't know if it mattered to anyone at any moment whether or not I existed.

Tatiana was at that lodge offering introductory thirty-minute sessions of her energy work. *Energy work.* I had no idea what that meant. But as the rain drizzled down outside, as I held myself in an endless shiver, I didn't care. I would take half an hour with anyone doing anything for me.

I went up to her room and sat in front of her while she closed her eyes, muttered to herself, waved her hands around, and shook them out in a bowl of water.

*This woman is crazy*, I thought. *None of this is going to help me. My heart. My poor heart.*

But five minutes in, something shifted. Not just for that moment, but possibly for the rest of my life. I had this wonderful thought:

*This woman is putting all of her effort and intention on me, a stranger, in this musty room on the coast. It's only half an hour. Give it a chance.*

I gave it a chance. I left that room feeling more open. A foot in the door of my heart, at least. A week later I went back to her for a full session. I lied down on a table while she did her work on the other side of the room. I felt a thawing. I cried for the first time in all that heartbreak. Actual tears, real gushing ones, after having felt like my chest was an immovable cinder block of pain. I walked home from that session and could see all the flowers blooming in shades I hadn't noticed. Someone was driving past me and stopped in the middle of the street to talk to me. We ended up going on a date, and I thought for the first time in months that it was possible that I was lovable.

"We are all way more psychic than we think," Tatiana said during one of those first sessions. "We pick up on other people's emotions and think they belong to us, but they don't." Those words still ring in my head and I think, *Really? Can that be true?* I remember as a child having the ability to emotionally understand a situation without any physical confirmation, yet I always doubted my feelings and kept looking for proof. Slowly, tragically, I stopped listening to that intuition. Tatiana taught me the concept of *clairsentience*, or the ability to know the emotional tenor of a room or a person just be sensing it, without having a conversation about it.

How liberating to know we have the tools inside us for our own healing. How generous of someone like Tatiana to teach other people to do the work themselves, instead of cultivating some mysterious air of an untouchable divine talent that others could never have.

This energy work that I once had no context for understanding, I now see how vital it is.

At another low point in my life (it's always the low points when we seek out healers) I came to Tatiana again.

"How has your week been?" she asked.

"Oh it's alright," I said. "It's just. I'm trying to be productive, but I keep getting stuck dealing with my emotions."

"Well," she said, "Dealing with our emotions is the primary reason we are here on Earth."

That is not a notion I ever found supported in my social spheres. We all have the feeling that we're not doing enough, we're not at the right job, we're not working hard enough to earn our keep. The idea that it is enough just to be here, to go through this, to laugh and cry at it all, that has given me such grace.

I owe Tatiana my life. I am proud to help her prepare this book for publication. This is important stuff and I thank you for taking the time to learn about it.


—Nick Jaina
Portland, Oregon

# THIS IS FOR YOU

This book is dedicated to you and your desire to create beauty and peace for yourself and your world.

It is infused with the energy of victory over your social conditioning and healing of your trauma.

Just having this book in your field will feel supportive because it is filled with love and recognition *for* you and *of* you.

Use it as you see fit to strengthen your practice of returning to the truth of you as already perfect.

Lightworker Training is a choose-your-own-adventure.

There are infinite depths of your being to explore, therefore the path of training yourself as a lightworker has no end.

This book is designed to be a guide and an inspiration, containing a manual of techniques as well as a story of initiation and continued travel on the path.

Everything in your life contains a possibility for deepening your practice of self-mastery.

You have the ability to remember and liberate the powerful, all-knowing, creative force within you.

This book contains the awareness of the truth that we must all do our own work and that we are never truly doing it alone.

May it inspire you to share the power of your love and light when you feel it and call you back to a remembrance of it when you don't.

# PART ONE

## CONCEPTS + CONSCIOUSNESS TOOLS

## Welcome

this is an initiation
this is the spark

of a new beginning
a deeper exploration

into the light
of creation
that you be

feel your breath and
feel this moment

acknowledge
your willingness
to begin again

feel your breath
and acknowledge
you are
right here
right now

welcome, lightworker
welcome home
to your self
as the power
and the presence of love

# CHAPTER 1:
# INITIATION

*Once you see the light you are, you can't un-see it*

## WHAT IS LIGHTWORKER TRAINING?

Lightworker Training is a series of lessons that can teach you how to work with the light and energy of creation. Together the lessons compose a well-rounded toolkit that distills essential teachings from myriad modalities.

The training will provide you with key concepts and structures for working with the power of your mind to direct the light of your energy and consciousness in a practical way. It includes instruction in mental foundations of effective lightwork practice, tools to develop your intuitive skills, and techniques for all essential steps in a lightwork session for yourself, a loved one, or a client.

Each chapter corresponds to a weekly lesson. Each week you can learn and practice a new set of tools. I have found a week to be the perfect balance of enough time to fully integrate and practice without feeling overwhelmed, but not so much that one loses momentum or starts forgetting what one has learned. That being said, you should work at the pace that suits you.

In **Part One**, you'll get a breakdown of the mindset and of the consciousness tools that are key to a foundational understanding of true healing. With these tools it is possible to make a top-down shift from the mental level that will affect the energetic, emotional, and physical bodies. Without these tools, you would simply be working at the level of symptoms and not getting to the root causes.

Without a shift in the mind, energy work becomes mechanical and lacks any lasting effects, but when the foundational mindset is engaged, the work becomes light and powerful. Instead of depleting your energy, it will nourish and uplift you.

In **Part Two**, you'll get a multimodality energy work toolkit. Tools are presented in the order in which they are typically performed in a lightwork session, from opening invocation to closing gratitude. Each chapter of **Part Two** corresponds with another step in the Lightwork Session Protocol outline that is given in the appendix.

To remind, inspire, and guide you, each chapter ends with a summary of Key Points, some Integration Tips to help you weave that chapter's tools and concepts into your daily life, and Practicum Possibilities that provide more structured exercises you can use to explore your understanding of the course and your personal journey of healing.

## WHERE DID IT COME FROM?

The tools I'm sharing were gathered through many channels: initiation through life experience, experimentation in personal practice, studying books, attending classes, meditation and contemplation, training with teachers and facilitators, countless hours of volunteer service, trading with other healers, sudden inspiration, working with hundreds of clients in thousands of sessions, facilitating ceremonial and educational events, teaching classes, receiving spiritual downloads, and other mysterious ways that I am unaware of, but grateful for nonetheless.

Every one of those beings and circumstances were my teachers. What I offer incorporates wisdom from many different schools. I encourage you to do what I did and take what works, make it yours, and don't worry about the rest. Don't take anything I say for granted, but rather notice what feels true for you. The truth is within you already, and when something aligns with that truth, you will feel it resonate like a bell being struck.

**Truth is not something you learn. It's something you remember that you already know.**

Because all the true and helpful teachings are divine reminders that belong to all and echo through our shared mind over and over until we all awaken to truth, it is impossible for any one individual to own them. Therefore, I claim no ownership over the wisdom of the teachings or the techniques that have been shared with me through my teachers. I claim ownership only of my unique presentation of them.

The empowerment, knowledge, and freedom that come from these practices are our birthright. Any wisdom you gain is thanks to spirit flowing through me and any errors are no doubt of my own ego identification. I am grateful for your forgiveness of them.

## WHY THIS BOOK?

This book is something that Lightworker Training students have been requesting for years, because no text currently exists to which I can refer them for study or reference. Like all my work, it is a synergy of many different teachings and I realize that much of what I present here may have been said before or even better by someone else, but we each bring our unique expression to our work, so this encourages me to keep going.

In this text, I share what I've found to be the most essential consciousness tools and energy work techniques to save time spent in suffering and to care for yourself and others, presented in a clear, ordered structure.

## PRINCIPLES OF LIGHTWORKER TRAINING

Lightworker Training is a collection of tools for empowerment and self-discovery. It is for those dedicated to self-love and self-realization who desire their lives be a positive contribution to the whole of life. It affirms that we are all co-creators of our experiences and that we are the only person we can free from suffering. There is no one else to free, because ultimately, we are one.

Lightworker Training affirms that you are a sovereign being of light and that the truth is already within you. Your natural state of being is one of abundant peace, knowledge, and freedom. You already have the ability to undo your social conditioning and return to the truth of your organic nature, which is powerful and free. Lightworker Training teaches you how to access what you already have.

Lightworker Training affirms that miracles are natural and healing of any kind is possible. It also recognizes that attachment to the form the healing takes could limit the possibilities experienced. It also recognizes that you can free yourself from limiting beliefs and the energetic residue of trauma and social conditioning.

Lightworker Training affirms that what heals one heals all and that you have the power within you to change your mind, your life, and your world.

Lightworker Training is a spiritual teaching, but it is non-hierarchical and non-dogmatic in nature. It is not an ideological program or belief system to subscribe to or reject. It is a multimodality toolkit based on the ancient art and science of spiritual practices that work with the organic light information of the unified field of consciousness.

Lightworker Training concepts and practices do not require or demand your belief in anything. As a matter of fact, it teaches practices through which, eventually, all beliefs are released. The truth is the truth and does not require anyone's belief in it, rather it will naturally make itself evident to those who are willing to know it.

Lightworker Training abides in spiritual minimalism and does not advocate for amassing a collection of physical tools. The only tool required is your mind. Even the energy work tools are simplified as much as possible while still teaching diverse applications.

Lightworker Training recognizes and honors the sovereignty of every being. Therefore, receiving explicit consent is essential before venturing into another's psychic or energetic space. If you find yourself judging another as needing your help, the most helpful thing you can do is to clear your own judgments about the person's situation so that you can see them as already perfect.

Those requesting healing service must be willing to let go of their attachments. This is true whether you are working with yourself or with another. You cannot take something from someone who is not willing to release it. They will use their free will to recreate it. Everyone must take responsibility for their own learning, healing, and spiritual growth.

As a sovereign being, responsible for your own learning, healing, and development, you get to say "yes" to that which resonates in alignment with what you'd like to create, and you get to say "no" to anything that doesn't. That includes anything I may offer in this course.

The techniques and practices given in this text are a complement to, not a replacement for, other forms of therapeutic treatments.

## HOW TO GET THE MOST OUT OF THIS WORK

My part in this work is to create a clear distillation of my extensive experience and present it to you in the form of helpful tools that you can easily learn. Your part is to use them.

Practice what works for you. This text means nothing without your experience of the tools. It is not enough to grasp a concept intellectually. Practice is essential. When you come to a section in the text that involves an experiential practice, take the time to actually do the steps. With that in mind, it is helpful to read this text when you are in a space that is conducive to practicing the techniques. Even the consciousness tools must be applied in a practical way to be meaningful.

**It's one thing to know and another to act like you know.**

If you are serious about mastering this work, I strongly encourage you to commit to it like you would a regular class. Go so far as to schedule study and practice time. Put times on your calendar and stick with them. Set an alert on your phone to remind you. Practice every day if possible. A short practice period of five minutes a day will preserve momentum and keep the material fresh in your mind. It will also accelerate your own healing process.

As you progress, you may wish to find a buddy with whom you can practice session work. You can even practice on a pet. Just make sure you get permission from whomever you'd like to work with.

It is helpful to have a dedicated notebook or journal for your studies. You might like to print a copy of the **Lightwork Session Protocol** and **Chakra Chart** pages to write notes on. You might prefer to draw your own. Some students have embellished their journal notes by adding drawings, writing with different colored pencils or pens, and attaching relevant found articles or images.

Your notebook can be a valuable reference tool during sessions, too. Yes, during sessions it is perfectly acceptable to look at your notes. Don't be shy about consulting them. As you progress through the material of the course, there are a few other physical tools you might like to make or acquire, like a spray smudge for energy hygiene. Those options will be discussed as they become relevant, but please know that your mind is the only tool you really need in order to do this work.

## BEING A BEGINNER

It is helpful to remember that when you first begin a new practice, you will most likely not be very adept at it. You may not always feel as though you are in the flow. You may feel a lack of confidence in your ability and comprehension. This is part of the process of learning something new and it is completely natural. It's also part of you developing trust. Trust in yourself. Trust in your ability. Trust that you can and are doing the work. Trust that it is working.

When I first started working with the tools presented in this text, I struggled with trust a lot. I had a deeply ingrained mental habit of tending to overthink and worry. The hyper-intellectual mind that was great for problem solving was also great at creating problems and endless hypothetical arguments that resulted in inaction and anxiety. Thankfully, I learned that I could divest all the mental energy I had spent focusing on what I *wouldn't* like to happen and instead invest it in focusing on what I *would* like to happen.

I also learned that the part of my mind that was worrying was trying to control situations because it felt disempowered. It was doing its best to avoid the kind of traumatic events that had occurred in the past, but it was operating from a place of fear. I learned that there was another mindstate I could access that felt powerful and peaceful. When I was willing to let love be in charge I was able to access that mindstate.

Little by little, as we experiment, we learn that we can trust in a love-led mindstate. It can reliably—and seemingly magically—come up with the perfect thing at the perfect time. Through it, we can experience more synchronicity and flow.

But even with so many breakthroughs, we still experience moments of not being in the flow. Moments when we listen to our fearful or ego-based thoughts instead of our true guidance. Moments when we worry about things instead of surrendering them to spirit. Moments when we become obsessed, confused, and conflicted. Moments when we doubt ourselves.

Through these useful demonstrations of contrasting causes and effects, we gain clarity in how to know and trust our true self, which is empowered through its connection to everything through the unified field of consciousness. We also learn how untrustworthy our false sense of self is, and that it is disempowered through fear and separation.

Acting through the guidance of the true self always results in positive out-comes and general feelings of peacefulness and empowerment, just as acting on fearful thoughts invariably leads to more lessons learned the hard way through pain and suffering. Contrast is a tremendously helpful learning device. Even so-called mistakes are helpful learning devices.

The development of trust is an essential aspect of this training specifically, and of spiritual practice in general. It takes repetitive demonstration of practices and principles to build trust in yourself. It is similar to building strength in a muscle. If you are new to an exercise, you will feel shaky at first, but as you practice over and over, you become increasingly strong in your faith. It is a faith in yourself and your ability. Little by little, you will achieve mastery over self-doubt and learn that you are completely trust-worthy when you are identified with your true nature. That true nature, of course, is love.

## ACHIEVING MASTERY

Ultimately, mastery means *self*-mastery. There is no one else, no *thing* else to master. All paths of learning lead to knowing and being your authentic self by stripping away anything that is not that. This is liberating.

On the path to mastery, you may start by practicing the tools your teachers have given you, but eventually you will transcend technique all together. This is what all masterful artists do: they begin with the structure of strong foundational technique, and then they create beyond those structures to ex-perience more of the infinite possibility of communing directly with Great Mystery.

The fastest way to mastery is to simply practice a little bit every day. Bring the tools, the new ways of thinking, the epiphanies, and the awareness into your daily life. Allow the mundane world to be illuminated by your con-sciousness a little bit more each day. Allow the barrier that separates your spiritual practice from the rest of your life to dissolve. Allow your true self to be seen and to be freed, little by little. Allow the process to unfold in its own perfect timing. Be compassionate and patient with yourself. We are all works in progress. Little by little, your life will become a work of art.

The practice of the art of your life will gently free you from the limitation and suffering of your mistaken beliefs and judgments. You will start to shine more of the natural light of your being and that light will start to shift and heal all aspects of your life: your body, your mind, your work, your relationships and your communities. The practice of your art will become a touchstone for you in moments of temporary confusion and despair. The darkness will lose its power over you, because once you see the beautiful light you are, you can't un-see it.

## YOU ARE THE TEACHER

One of the primary goals of Lightworker Training is to help you to recognize and receive the guidance of the ever-present teacher you have within you. We all have a wise aspect of our being that speaks, usually softly, through symbols, feelings, synchronicity, and sometimes even through other people or external sources.

We learn eventually that the inner teacher's voice is the only voice worth giving our attention to, because we realize that it is guiding us from a place of total love and its only interest is our happiness. With practice, you will be able to discern this voice for love and receive its guidance clearly and consistently.

The inner teacher is your own intuition. It is right there in the word itself. *In*-tuition means inner teaching. We all have the ability to access through our intuition, but we perhaps lack experience in the practice of doing so. In Lightworker Training we are learning how to tune into sources of subconscious, energetic, and spiritual information.

Practice is key. Ultimately, you can read all the books, take all the classes, and watch all the videos in the world, but it won't make any difference if you don't practice. Through your practice, you will gain trust in yourself and your intuition. You will become conversant in the language of spirit and you will recognize the voice of the inner teacher.

## AS FOR ME

Like any other helpful teacher, I may have been practicing these particular tools a bit longer, more intensively, or differently than you have, so I am able to share information based on my experiences that may be useful for you. I am not any more special than you are. My gifts are not any more powerful. I am not any more spiritual. In fact, I never imagined I would be doing this work. To illustrate my point, I'm going to share some of my story with you. Fair warning: some of it is pretty intense.

Part of the reason I became interested in traditional healing techniques was that I had many challenges during my life that affected my psychological and physical health. I was taken from my mother as a baby and put into foster care, eventually adopted by parents who took turns being psychologically and physically abusive. As a child I was prone to both life-threatening and chronic illnesses and accidents. As a teen I went on to develop patterns of antisocial behavior that grew into criminal acts, homelessness, substance addiction, and dysfunctional relationships that included physical and emotional abuse. During my young adulthood I was sexually molested and assaulted, stalked, beaten, stabbed and threatened at gunpoint. I've been hurt by people who said they loved me. I've been abandoned. I've literally been kicked when I was down.

It would be totally understandable if I was feeling damaged after all that and indeed I have struggled tremendously with multiple forms of obsession, addiction, anxiety, panic attacks, and depression. I've even tried to kill myself. It's a miracle that I'm still here, so trust me when I say that if I can do this healing work, you can too. My life is testimony that you can heal yourself and that the tools I present here are not only effective, but can dramatically heal every aspect of your life.

The reason I have total confidence in your ability to learn and master the tools I am presenting here is because I know we are both extensions of the same organic light of universal consciousness. We are equally capable of working with the light of our being. We are equally capable of knowing the truth. Knowledge is not something that is discovered outside of ourselves. Rather it is revealed, through clearing of psychic clutter, as something that has always been within. No matter how dark the dark night of the soul, we all have the ability to find our way back to the light of our true selves. In fact, sometimes the darkest, most desperate times will lead us that much more quickly to discovering our true nature. It was because of the most painful experience in my life that I came to discover and be interested in learning about energy work.

In early 2007, after a week of the most severe headaches I had ever experienced, I was turned away for MRIs at an emergency room because I didn't have insurance. A day later I was hospitalized with a life-threatening MRSA infection in my eye socket. By the time I was admitted I was almost beyond help. It took another several days for the very large and continuous doses of opiates I was given to even slightly curb the pain. During those first few excruciating days, something happened that changed my life, but I wouldn't fully recognize it until much later.

I think it was the third night I was in the hospital. Time had no meaning. I was in a state of seemingly endless suffering. I was drifting in and out of consciousness in a shared room with three other women who I couldn't see but could hear behind the curtains that separated our hospital beds. At one point in the night I woke up to a maddening pain and I could hear moans of anguish from the woman in the bed next to me. Across the room another woman was struggling to breathe through a respirator. I couldn't hear the third woman across from me, but I could feel her. The air was thick with collective pain and despair.

I closed my eyes again and suddenly became aware that there were two other beings in the room with me. Their presence was real, but I could also tell that they weren't in a physical form. I could see them clearly even though my eyes were closed. The fact that I wasn't surprised at all by them was itself surprising. They were dressed like ninjas, all in black. Their energy was calm and clear. I recognized them at once as masters, and I simultaneously wondered how that could possibly be.

They told me it was my turn now, which I also simultaneously understood and didn't understand. The part of me that understood focused inward and started to breathe in the most slow, expansive, and loving way I had ever breathed. I had used yoga-type breath regulation before to help me calm down when I was having panic attacks, but this was a breath beyond what I thought was even possible. It was more loving than anything I had ever felt. As I was breathing this loving breath, I became aware of a tiny point of pure, brilliant white light within me. I focused all my attention on it, mentally diving into this tiny point of light at the center of my being until I was immersed in it.

In the light there was no pain. There was only a peace beyond comprehension. I continued to focus on the light. I was in it and it was in me. With each slow, focused, loving breath, I could feel the light grow bigger and brighter inside of me. It radiated through my whole body until my body was filled with light and peace.

I got lighter and lighter. I kept breathing and I could feel my light expanding out past the edges of my body and into the room, rippling out on the waves of my breath to fill the space—and as it did I felt it dissolve all of the heaviness. The moans of pain and gasping breath started to diminish. I felt the light radiating through everything, through the other women, dissolving their pain and filling them with peace. I could feel their breathing shift and slow to come into alignment with mine. And I could feel the rhythmic waves of all of us breathing together as one.

Sounds pretty miraculous, right? Well, it was, but it was also so natural that I didn't really think about it at all afterward. Granted, I was in such a physical state that it literally took all of my energy just to keep my body alive, but it still amazes me how perfectly natural miracles can be.

After several months of home care, when I was back out in the world again (with two functioning eyes, no less), I was suddenly taken with the idea that I had to learn energy work even though I had no idea what that meant. Thus started an adventure down a mysterious path I never thought I'd travel, following the breadcrumb trail of energy, wherever it might lead.

Just as I never thought I would be doing lightwork for a living, I definitely never thought I would be teaching it, let alone writing a book about it. I love teaching because I love learning, and teaching is a way to learn more. Sharing knowledge is like all expressions of love in that the more you share, the more you have. I invite you to share these teachings as you feel inspired to do so. You might be surprised by what you discover you already know.

## CHAPTER 1 :: KEY POINTS

- You are a sovereign being of light.
- The truth is already within you.
- Your natural state of being is one of abundant peace, knowledge, and freedom.
- You have the ability to undo your social conditioning and return to the truth of your organic nature, which is powerful and free.
- Miracles are natural.
- Healing is possible.
- You can free yourself from limiting beliefs and the energetic residue of trauma.
- You have the power within you to change your mind, your life, and your world.

## CHAPTER 1 :: INTEGRATION TIPS

- Throughout the day, remind yourself that there is a point of light within you that is infinitely vast, loving, and peaceful. Try putting a screen saver image on your phone or a note somewhere that helps remind and inspire you.
- Integrate something that feels loving and nurturing into your daily routine, like eating a healthy meal, saying a prayer, taking some deep breaths, spritzing yourself with rosewater, or taking a salt bath. Create small self-love rituals. Start with small steps and stick to it.
- Cultivate gratitude. Say "thank you" to your breath. Give thanks for the water as you wash your dishes or take a shower. Thank the earth for the food, clothing, and shelter. Thank all the beings that make life possible and

interesting. Thank the people that have upset you for teaching you more about yourself. Thank yourself for being willing to be thankful. Try putting thank you notes on your fridge or faucets, on your phone, on your desk or in your car to remind you to feel grateful.

## CHAPTER 1 :: PRACTICUM POSSIBILITIES

**Intention setting:** (5 - 10 minutes)

Get your journal or notebook and write out some intentions for what you'd like to accomplish or receive from this training. What are you interested in? What is your focus? Is there something you'd like to change in your life? What are the challenges? What tools would be helpful? What are you excited about?

**Toolkit inventory:** (10 - 15 minutes)

Write in your journal a list of the healing tools you already possess. For example, are you intuitive, compassionate, caring, sensitive? Do you know how to help yourself or others feel more loved, more grounded, or clearer? Do you know some ways of clearing energies? List as many things as you can. Are you surprised by how much you already know? Did something come up that you forgot about or were able to see in a different light?

**Shadow inventory:** (as long as you like)

Take some time to reflect on the shadow aspects of yourself and your experience that you are bringing to this work. Remember how I listed some of the dark moments of my life in the section about me? All of those seemingly horrible things ended up being food for my spiritual practice and helped make me as strong as I am today. They have helped me to have great compassion for others and myself. They have taught me valuable skills. And although incredibly painful to go through, I am at a place now where I am genuinely grateful for the benefit of the learning received. So for this exercise, I invite you to write in your journal a list of shadow aspects and experiences with an intention of discovering some of your hidden strengths and abilities. Take as long as you like. Please know that working with shadow can bring up all kinds of trapped emotions, memories, and feelings in the body. Go at a pace that feels graceful for you and take time to process anything that comes up for healing.

Remember, all that is required for miraculous healing is your willingness to receive the gift of what is arising and let go of the rest.

If a lot of emotions and energy are coming up for release, take time to be with the feelings, let them flow through you, drink lots of water, take a salt bath if you like, and rest.

# You are already perfect

would you affirm
your brokenness
by trying to fix it?

I invite you to take a breath

imagine
grounding yourself
in knowing
there is nothing to do

you are already rooted in
foundational wisdom

breathe and remember
the truth of you
is older
than the stones of the mountain

be still and observe
the sensations in your body

in the stillness you will know
the crystalline perfection
of yourself and all beings

# CHAPTER 2:
# FOUNDATIONS OF HEALING

*In stillness you will know the truth of yourself*

## WHAT IS HEALING?

Everything is useful in the sense that we can learn from it. Everything can be used as grist for the spiritual mill, and that is a blessing. But what about awareness and practices that can save us time spent grinding away? Is there something that can accelerate our learning or make it more graceful?

Yes, definitely. In a word, it's love. You could also call it non-judgment, presence, or unity consciousness. The word I prefer to use for this energy/consciousness is love.

Love is healing. It is the foundation of all truly helpful practices and you don't have to figure out how to get it, because love is your natural state of being. Love is natural, so healing is natural.

By its very nature, love is unconditional. Like the sun shines and the rain falls on everyone regardless of who or what or where, love is extended to all equally. It responds to all requests in the same way, with love. Sometimes its response is tender, sometimes fierce, but always it is grounded in calm power and clear purpose.

The power of love is only accessible in the present moment, because the present moment is all that exists. Love reminds you that you are worthy of love. Actually, it reminds you that you can't be unworthy of it because you *are* it.

Love also reminds us that we are one with the larger organism of all of life. If we attune to its frequency, we can feel that love, a force of nature that is flowing through us and through all things.

When you recognize that the essence of you as the power of love is already perfect, you will experience healing.

## WHAT DOES IT MEAN TO HOLD SPACE?

Holding space means staying vigilant for love. It means remembering the truth of you as perfect love, even in the midst of fearful feelings, perceived problems, attack thoughts, physical ailments, mental chaos, and emotional discord.

When upsetting events or thoughts about events trigger upsetting feelings, it can be challenging to even be willing to hold space for healing, but it only takes an instant of willingness to release anything that doesn't allow you to know and feel the peace of your love. In that conscious instant, you can pause, take a breath, get grounded in love, and choose to experience something else.

Holding space invokes trust that on some level you are okay. That on some level everyone and everything is okay. That you can release anything that gets in the way of feeling okay. That you can tap into the intelligence of the larger organism for help. That you can and will heal and learn. That you are a force of nature.

Holding space means to surrender. It requires relinquishment of all attach-ment to the outcome. You aim the arrow of your intention toward the target and you let go. You offer your gifts to someone else and you let go. You offer your service to the world and you let go.

Holding space involves wisdom. Wisdom to know that you can only control what thoughts you cultivate in your mind and what choices you make. Acknowledging that you can't control other people's choices or the outcome of anything. Knowing what you are and aren't responsible for is liberating and empowering for everyone.

Holding space ultimately empowers you and everyone else. If you feel drained, exhausted, martyred, or resentful, you are missing some key piece of holding space. You may be holding a belief that you are responsible for other people's emotions or wellness or making them responsible for yours.

Holding space requires calm, grounded energy, alive with spirit and power and purpose. It requires balance and compassionate non-attachment. It requires the willingness to be the space. The space of infinite possibility, mystery and grace.

Holding a loving space is healing in and of itself. It is helpful to maintain this kind of loving presence, not only in healing work, but as a way of life. The more you can cultivate the mindfulness of loving presence in your daily life, the more you will accelerate your learning and healing journey.

## MINDFULNESS

Perhaps instead of "mindfulness" it should be called "mind emptiness," because truly being mindful requires being present, and we can't be present if our minds are cluttered with thoughts of what just happened (also known as the past) or what is about to happen (aka the future).

Consider for a moment how many thoughts you have that are only about what is happening right now. If you're anything like me, you may be shocked to realize that most of your mental energy is spent on things that already happened or haven't happened yet and very little is paid to what is actually happening now. There is something to be said for reflection and planning, but there is also something we can observe in how much mental energy we invest in fruitless ventures.

Perhaps you can relate to the following examples of how my mental chaos has manifested:

• I have exhausted myself and spent entire days trying to figure out possible futures, my mind spinning and weaving scenarios that didn't get me any closer to a resolution.
• I've spent countless hours ruminating on past events with my ego operating as lawyer, accused, and judge, as it gathered evidence, presented cases for and against, proclaimed my innocence or guilt and doled out punishment for my so-called offenses.
• I have tormented myself with the guilt of unloving thoughts, the pain of unloving interpretations of other people's actions, and the shame of finding myself lacking in love.
• I have worried about future events and regretted past mistakes until it made me sick mentally, emotionally, and physically.

Like a person having a nightmare who doesn't understand that the torture they are experiencing is only in their mind, I didn't know that the anguish I was experiencing was based on completely made-up thoughts. I didn't understand that I had turned the power of my mind against myself like a weapon. If there was anyone who ever needed mind healing it was me.

The first and most helpful thing we can be aware of in practicing mindfulness is the difference between being caught up in our thoughts and being present. We can begin to notice things that are actually happening right now, instead of what we are thinking about. We can practice getting out of our heads and connecting with the body. We can take time to pause, breathe deeply, and feel, notice, and listen.

Try this practice for about thirty seconds:

• Close your eyes.
• Feel your body breathe.
• Feel the clothes and the air on your skin.
• Listen to all the layered sounds around you.

(Go ahead and try it right now. I'll wait for you.)


...................................


Notice if anything has shifted energetically. What are you feeling now?

During the practice of present moment awareness perhaps you become aware of the process of thinking, watching yourself think, noticing the thoughts you are thinking. Maybe you tune into the sensations you are feeling in your body, whether they are comfortable or uncomfortable. Maybe you notice a lack of feeling. Any and all of these are simple yet profoundly useful approaches. And the really amazing thing is that it doesn't matter what you feel, if anything.

That's right—it doesn't matter if you get present and don't notice anything. Or if you notice you feel great or terrible. It doesn't matter if you feel totally disconnected and like a complete loser. It doesn't matter if you feel like an ascended master.

It's not your observed state that is empowering or healing, it's your willingness to observe it.

Getting present in and of itself is helpful regardless of what your experience of the practice is. Simply checking in with yourself, noticing what is actually happening right now in your mind, your emotions, and your body, is healing. It's a wonderful way to be there for yourself and build stronger communication with aspects of the mind/body complex, which has much to share with you.

Your body, like that of all animals, lives in the present. When you are present with your body, your body will feel more at ease and you will be able to receive more of the rich information it is constantly sharing with you. When you are present with your emotions, you will feel less rocked by their waves and be able to roll more gracefully with their ebb and flow. You will also learn what they have to teach you. When you are present with your thoughts you will learn more about your conditioned beliefs, your mind, and how it works. With more of this valuable awareness comes more possibility for choice. And after a while, believe it or not, you will even begin to choose which thoughts you think. All of that is possible when you dwell in the present.

## THE SIGNIFICANCE OF UNRESOLVED TRAUMA

What takes us out of awareness of the present moment are all the distracting thoughts that come in the form of our anxiety, worries, fears, obsessions, depressions, and ruminations. Major distractions that block us from being deeply in tune with the present are almost always based on a foundation of unresolved trauma and the patterns of a central nervous system that gets stuck in a state of fight, flight, or freeze in an attempt to keep our bodies alive.

I've yet to meet anyone that doesn't have some unresolved trauma energy lurking around somewhere. Even folks who haven't knowingly experienced first-hand traumatic events can be carrying old trauma from something repressed, witnessed, or inherited. It could even be something multidimensional.

If you take these aspects into consideration and just imagine briefly the ways humans have been terrorizing themselves and each other for millennia, you start to get an appreciation for how deeply ingrained in our very DNA some of these ancient unresolved trauma energies could be. You might even start to have compassion for some of the crazy-seeming brain and body triggers that appear to sideswipe you out of nowhere.

One of the interesting things about trauma is that it tends to cascade and compound, meaning that when the mind/body is triggered by a current situation that is traumatic it tends to trigger body memories of the old traumas as well. If it seems like your response to something is totally out of proportion to what is actually happening in the present moment, you are probably experiencing old trauma energy being triggered.

For example, several years ago I was living with a roommate who was even more anal about housekeeping than me. As much as I loved him, his personality could be overbearing at times. One day, I filled up the electric kettle and turned it on to make tea when he said, "I was going to use that hot water to make rice."

I was confused. "There wasn't any hot water in there."

He suddenly got very angry. The anger was evident not so much in his voice, but rather as a deep burning rage in his eyes as he glared at me and said, "Yes. There. Was."

As soon as I felt his anger, my whole body flooded with emotions. My face flushed. I felt ashamed, afraid, nauseous, and anxious. My mind became confused. I felt like I was spiraling into some hellish abyss.

"I swear, there wasn't. There wasn't any water in there," I stuttered. What was I saying? Why was I arguing this point? Why couldn't I just say "sorry" and move on? It felt like my life depended on him believing me.

A moment later, I had a clear, visceral memory of the time when I was eight years old and I accidentally came home without my math book. I had let a girl on the bus check it out and forgot to get it back before we got off at our stops. She lived down the street. I could have gone to get it. But instead, I was beaten by my father who was inexplicably enraged by the fact that I didn't have the book.

That day in the kitchen with my roommate and our electric tea kettle, I realized that that long-distant traumatic event from my past was still very present. It was there, imprinted in my body and brain, just waiting to be triggered in full emotional technicolor realness.

That day I had an epiphany in which I saw clearly why I had always felt such urgency around proving that I was right and why simple mistakes had devastated me for so many years. It wasn't because I was an egotistical perfectionist as I had previously assumed. It was because my brain was trying desperately to save my body from incurring the wrath of violent outbursts and further trauma. I could also see the pattern of how my father's hurtful rage was caused by the unresolved trauma of the violence he witnessed and experienced in his childhood. I suspected that this was also the case for my roommate, but I didn't stick around much longer to find out.

At the time of the tea kettle incident, I didn't know exactly what to do with any of that trauma information just yet, but from that moment on, I was aware of the fact that my childhood trauma was very much alive and unwell. From that moment on, I was able to start to have more compassion for my mental patterns of anxiety, control, and obsession. I was able to see it all as a desire for safety, and a cry for love. I started to cultivate the willingness to answer that cry not with more self-loathing, but with the only sane answer I could give—compassion.

You may notice I said I was willing to respond with love. It took a tremendous amount of practice to begin to rewire my brain, start healing the old trauma energies, and be able to unconditionally love myself even a little bit. But it all started with my willingness.

Are you willing?

## LET'S TAKE A BREATH

Whew! Trauma is intense! Sometimes I wish I could wave a magic wand and heal everyone on this planet, but that wouldn't work because it's up to each one of us to learn our Earth School lessons.

What I *can* do is share what I've learned, based on personal experience from my own life and from witnessing my clients' processes.

I can share the tools I've found that save time spent in suffering.

I can share my deep knowingness that you can heal anything. You can rewire your brain. You can retrain your nervous system.

You can release the heaviness of fear-based beliefs and survival responses.

Whether they are yours, your ancestors, or the collective's, you can heal them. And it will get easier as you practice.

You will reclaim your ability to feel safer, more grounded, more present, and better able to respond to what is arising.

You're already doing it.

Luckily, the way is very simple and clear. We'll get into the hows in a minute, but first a bit more on understanding trauma energies so that we can be compassionate with our process.

## THE BODY AND TRAUMA

I feel it is important to talk about trauma energy because of its pervasiveness and because it is very possible that as you are reading this book or going through your healing process and practices you will encounter something that triggers a trauma memory in your body. I invite you to remember that every time a trauma memory gets triggered in the body, it is an opportunity for deep healing.

When trauma energy is triggered, the brain is picking up on some stimulus that it associates with a traumatic event from the past. To your brain, the stimulus equals something that endangers your body's well-being or ability to survive, so it shifts gears and activates the sympathetic nervous system. The sympathetic state of arousal then responds with either a fight, flight, or freeze strategy to deal with the trauma trigger of feeling unsafe.

When your body goes into fight or flight survival mode, a couple things happen which are helpful to keep in mind. The brain control switches from the prefrontal cortex zone of rational thought and cognition to the amygdala zone of primal animal survival. That means you won't be thinking clearly. You'll be hyper alert and subconsciously aware of a million tiny details of your surroundings, but your body will be responding to these stimuli without thinking.

The body may feel like it is on autopilot and you can't control it. This is actually helpful in a true life-or-death situation in which you literally don't have time to think. When you're in a circumstance in which pausing to think could cost you your life, your body's amazing subconscious powerhouse needs to take over and get things done fast. But when you're just trying to live your life—like maybe making yourself a cup of tea at home—and unresolved trauma suddenly gets triggered, it can feel frustrating to say the least.

When the trigger hits, you may suddenly be filled with anger (the energy of fight), fear (the energy of flight), or shock (the energy of freeze). Your breath becomes fast and shallow. Blood and energy rushes from your brain and organs to your major muscle groups for said fighting or fleeing, which means less for the brain and less for fine motor skills. You may feel like you're fumbling both mentally and physically and that is absolutely the case.

Not incidentally, when your body is in the sympathetic mode of fight or flight, it is not only unable to think clearly, it is also unable to properly digest food, rest, relax, sleep, or heal. For those crucial functions to happen, it must switch out of sympathetic survival mode and into the parasympathetic mode of rest and digest.

Both the sympathetic and parasympathetic modes are helpful. Once you understand them a bit more and how they work, you can be aware of what state you are in and consciously make a shift.

Yes, you can consciously make a shift, which is essential for your healing, because much of our modern way of life increases the stress under which our bodies are operating. The electronic devices that surround us, the numerous electromagnetic fields in our environment that disturb our bodies' natural biofields, the tremendous amount of violence we are exposed to through our entertainment choices, and the constant bombardment of advertising designed to be jarringly loud and bright are but a few of the many things that place additional stress on our bodies by triggering sympathetic nervous system arousal and thereby keeping us in a low-grade state of survival energy almost all day long.

I say this not to induce feelings of overwhelm or despair, but to illustrate that there could be a very sane reason why you might feel crazy. When your body and brain don't get enough quality parasympathetic time, it can lead to innumerable health issues, both mental and physical.

In my personal and professional practice, I have seen trauma energies at the root cause of almost every major challenge people are facing—stress, anxiety, depression, fear of intimacy, addiction, self-destructive behaviors, mistrust of self and others, blocks to giving and receiving love and support, even chronic physical pain and fatigue. And I've found that if we get curious and look deeply into the causes of what shows up on the surface level as these symptoms, we tend to see that beneath it all is some unresolved trauma, usually compounded through a combination of inherited traits and social conditioning.

Can you see how many of the symptoms listed above could be ways to manage and cope with trauma? Can you see how those symptoms could be based on beliefs about what we must do to stay safe and avoid more trauma, pain, and suffering? And can you sense that there might be alternative ways to do this?

## REWRITING THE PROGRAMS OF FEAR

First, let's be clear: fear can be a gift when it is helping your body survive. Your body's survival tactics have worked for both your ancestors and you, because here you are, reading this. Congratulations, you made it!

Fear becomes unhelpful when we find ourselves in a near-constant state of sympathetic activation. This continuous low-grade fear and stress actually starts to erode our body's ability to survive and thrive. Balance, rest, and time to heal are crucial for our body's resilience and its ability to bounce back from traumatic events. So, how do we get more of that parasympathetic rest and digest time?

The simplest way to switch from sympathetic mode to parasympathetic mode is to breathe deeply. When your body is in sympathetic mode, breathing becomes shallow or the breath is held and muscles start to tense in anticipation of fighting or fleeing. By breathing deeply and relaxing the muscles as much as possible, we are sending a message to our bodies that says, "It's okay, you're safe."

Even in those rare cases where you might have to literally fight or flee, taking a deep breath and dropping your energy down into your belly will help you to stay as calm, grounded, and effective as possible. Martial artists are masters of being calm and centered under pressure.

Deep breathing is also a powerful way to discharge energy. If you are feeling nervous about something, try inhaling deeply and strongly through the nose and exhaling quickly with a forceful sound of rushing wind out through the mouth. You can also try yawning to discharge tension in the body. Animals do this all the time. In fact, if you want to calm an animal that is tense or nervous, a very effective method is to sit nearby without making eye contact, drop your breath down into your belly, get super present and still, relax your body, and yawn.

Your body is an animal, so it makes sense that if you want to discharge trauma energy, you can do what animals do: shake it off, yawn, breathe deeply, get still, and allow the body to reset.

When trauma is getting triggered, it's especially tricky to practice calming techniques, but the way to create a new pattern is to do something different than what you feel compelled to do in the moment. The more intense the trauma, the more challenging it will be and the more of a total badass you will be when you transform it.

What I am going to suggest you try is probably the exact opposite of what you'd like to do when you get triggered. When old trauma gets triggered, you may feel like you want to run away to the nearest bar, pound a few shots, then numb out further with some nachos, TV, or sex with strangers. Or perhaps you want to scream in someone's face while smashing one of their most prized body parts. Or perhaps you want to curl up in a ball and die because what's the point anyway. Perhaps you even want to hurt or harm your body because then at least *you'll* be in control of your pain.

Whatever form your trauma-triggered sympathetic state is manifesting as, my suggestion is going to be the same: try something completely different. Something that might be uncomfortable at first but ultimately empowering. The techniques are thankfully simple:

1. Pause.
2. Breathe.
3. Feel.

## STILLNESS AND LISTENING

When we pause and get still, we send a powerful message. We demonstrate that we are willing to hold space for ourselves. We signal to our bodies that they are safe and can heal. We express our interest in knowing the truth. We become one with the power and presence of ourselves as love.

When we tune in and listen to what our minds, bodies, and emotions are communicating to us, we automatically heal because we are demonstrating our unconditional love for ourselves.
In the stillness we affirm there is no other place to be, no other way to be. We affirm that we are seen and heard, that our cries for love and acknowledgement are answered, not with guilt, shame or blame, but with love and acceptance.

In listening, we demonstrate that we are willing to receive. We can listen for the truth. We can listen for the guidance of our wise inner teacher. We can receive the gifts of grace. We can hear the song of creation that all of nature is singing.

To sing, we must listen. To rise, we must dive deep. Deep within the present moment is a well of peace that defies explanation, a space infinitely tiny and vast, an eternal instant.

In the stillness, listening to the song of creation, we transcend whatever limitation appears in the world of form, and heal through all time and space.

## A FORCE OF NATURE

You are a force of nature. You are one with nature. It is not some place out-side of you that you visit on holidays and weekends. It is you.

The separation that most humans currently believe happened doesn't really exist. Because we think it exists, we experience the effects of that. More on that in the next chapter on mind, but for now, just know that you are an in-terdependent cell in the larger organism, and that organism has your back. You can tap into the intelligence that creates and sustains the universe, because you share it.

What benefits one cell benefits all cells. What is good for the organism is good for the cell, and vice versa. The universe supports you in being a happy, healthy cell. If you send a signal to the one mind we share, it will be answered and it is guaranteed that if you are willing to receive the answer, it is yours.

## THE PACE OF THE BODY

Every call for love is answered immediately, but sometimes the body takes time. Consciousness is everything, everywhere, all the time. Therefore it is instantaneous. Mental energy moves quickly, consequently we can shift it easily. Emotions go through a wave-like process that moves a bit slower. And the physical world is the densest energy of all, so it moves slower still.

That's not to say we can't shift physical reality quickly, because we definitely can. It's just that most physical symptoms did not manifest overnight and it can be gentler for the body to release that energy over time. The body knows what it's doing. Trust that it is healing in the perfect time. By releas-ing judgments of what you think its healing process should look like, you create more space for it to make the shift into wholeness.

When there is a lot of trauma energy, the body will only release what feels safe in any given moment, then it will go through a period of integration before it is ready to release more.

Integration can take a few minutes, a few weeks, or a few months. There is no right or wrong way or time to heal something.

Think about nature, of which you are a part. How nothing is rushed, yet miraculous change occurs every season. Change that is sustainable and powerful.

When we release our ideas about what healing should look like and the pace at which it unfolds, we release shame and open our selves to receive more of the healing power of love. This lightens our hearts and creates sustainability in our daily practices and resiliency in times of distress.

## THE HEALING POWER OF PRESENCE

The practice of present moment awareness is important because all the power that ever was or will be is here now. There is no other time/place to be. All the action is happening right here and now. If we aren't present we miss out on the experience of it. We won't be able to access our true power. We won't be aware of what is real, what is possible, what we know, or what choices we have. We won't be open to receiving guidance from our inner teacher or be able to follow our intuition. All of this is only accessible in the present moment.

Being totally present heals us. This is because presence is in alignment with our true nature. Truly, we are only ever here now and no other time or place. Anything in alignment with the truth of you is healing. Every choice to be your true, whole, sane self is an act of healing for you and everyone else, because we are all part of the same organism. The truth of you is love, light, consciousness, and power. It is grace, peace, strength, and knowing. It is infinite and eternal. It is here, everywhere, now, and forever.

I shared with you how I had an experience of myself in the hospital as an infinite being of light, totally present and focused. Once I was discharged, it didn't take long before I started slipping back into typical human fear and doubt, but something had shifted.

During the months I was recovering at home, I had little to distract me from noticing what was happening in my mind. This was a few weeks into my convalescence, and the physical pain had lessened to the point where my mind was able to think thoughts again. Because I had had a break from thinking, I was able to observe my mind differently than I had before. As I observed it, I learned something interesting: I was vacillating between two mindstates.

I saw that one of those mindstates was in total allowance of whatever was happening in the present moment. It was the same quiet, calm presence that had got me through the hospital ordeal. The other mindstate was anything but present. In fact, that mindstate seemed to have an extreme aversion to the present moment and a sick fascination with entertaining fearful thoughts, such as *what if my eye doesn't heal, what if I get Crohn's disease, what if the infection doesn't go away, what if the PICC line gets infected, what if I start throwing up again, what if I can't go back to work, what if, what if, what if?*

The "what if" game was exhausting.

But, because I was observing my mind and not identified as it, even in that exhausted place I knew that somehow I could get back to the first mindstate, the one of allowance and presence. I didn't always know how to get there, but I knew that in that state I could deal with anything that was arising. In the present moment, I knew what needed to be done and I could do it, no matter how difficult, how painful, how nauseating. There was comfort in that knowingness.

I began to understand the link between presence and peace. At first, I judged myself for all the time in my life I wasted by not being present. But then it eventually dawned on me: the present moment is *the only time that actually exists.* I felt liberated. I knew that any time I was thinking about the past or the future, I wasn't actually anywhere or doing anything. If it was true that the present is truly all that exists, then all my thoughts about the past or future were less than meaningless. They were nothing.

As I had more glimpses of present moment awareness, more was revealed.

I started to have a felt experience of the power of presence. Any time I wanted to be at peace, all I had to do was stop thinking and start being. All I needed were some deep breaths and the willingness to be present. I would close my eyes (or to be more exact, the one eye that wasn't already sewn shut) and feel my breath. I would feel the pain in my body and feel grateful that the pain was bearable, grateful for the medications that were supporting my body's healing, thankful for my bed, content to have clean sheets, cozy blankets, and a warm home in which to rest and recover.

When I was present, the simplest things I had taken for granted before became celebrated and appreciated. At meal times, I was aware of and thankful for all the beings that made my meal possible and how all those beings were supporting my body's healing. I chewed my food thoroughly and was grateful that my body could digest it. I thanked my body for all the amazing work it was doing.

Because of the pain and weakness I felt, even the smallest mundane tasks like bathing, cooking, or washing dishes took all my mental focus and physical strength. I would be absolutely present with each one of them, slowly and mindfully working through the steps of each part of the task, breathing, moving deliberately, and occasionally even becoming so absorbed in the moment that I would marvel at all the things that were working together to create indoor plumbing, electricity, and the hot water running through the soap suds on my hands.

All my senses were heightened. The bright color and pungency of the mustard greens in my eggs was invigorating. Tea was bracing. Coffee unthinkable. Sudden movements were to be avoided at all costs. I could see the rainbow colors in sunlight and hear the hum of electricity in the lights of the apartment. My body was throbbing with the beating of my heart. Every sensation was exquisitely bright and clear to the point of overwhelm. All I could do was breathe and move slowly, mindfully. One breath at a time.

In the constant state of sensory overwhelm that I inhabited in those days, I had no means of coping other than to practice being present and taking everything one breath at a time. In this forced state of mindfulness I wasn't able to focus on anything but the task at hand, which was helpful because when I shifted to being present, the worries and fears I had about not being able to clean the bathroom at that moment, not being able to be free of nausea and pain, not being able to earn money to pay for my expenses, along with a multitude of other fears, evaporated into nothingness.

I learned that total focus on the present was key. I learned how to focus my mind, not only when I was performing physical tasks, but also when I was resting. When I was focused and present, my mind was able to relax, which settled my emotions, which settled my body. By being present, I had found a way to comfort myself in a time that was physically exhausting and mentally challenging. It was so simple and perfect that it was easy to forget, but since I needed it so desperately at the time, luckily it was also easy to remember.

Those months of being at home with no distractions of work, social life, or activities gave me an amazing opportunity to go deep into a minute-by-minute, day-by-day mindfulness practice that has served me well ever since, but you don't have to get sick and spend months in constant pain and stressful recovery to learn what I did. You can practice intensive mindfulness right now and a great way to start building your presence muscle is through the act of meditation.

The following exercise is designed to help you have a felt experience of presence. Before trying the experiment, read through the instructions first, then give it a go.

Don't worry about the order of the specific steps or doing it right. Allow yourself to soak in the frequency of the intention.

## EXERCISE :: PRESENT MOMENT AWARENESS

For this exercise we will hold four points of focus intently to quiet our thoughts and become immersed in the present moment.

**1.** Find a comfortable position, either lying down or sitting. If you are sitting, shift your weight to find a place of balance with the spine straight and shoulders relaxed.

**2.** Let your belly be relaxed and breathe deeply and naturally.

**3.** Keeping the breath flowing, **focus on total stillness in the body**. Focus on not moving a muscle as you let your breath be natural.

**4.** Next, while maintaining body stillness, **hold your gaze on one point** and keep it totally still and relaxed. It's okay if the image focus softens and blurs as long as the eyes remain still.

**5.** Next, while maintaining still body and still gaze, **focus on listening** and soak in the soundscape, noticing the sounds all around, near and far. Open your awareness to all the layered sounds.

**6.** Next, while maintaining your focus on still body, still gaze, and focused listening, **focus on feeling** the sensations in the body. Notice where it feels comfortable or uncomfortable, notice the subtle sensations of energy moving, notice the feeling of your clothing, the movement of your breath.

**7.** Hold all points of focus (still body, still gaze, listening, feeling) for 30 seconds.

**8.** Release and notice what that felt like.

While you were holding all four points of focus intently, were you able to think about anything besides the present moment?

What does it feel like in your body now? In your mind?

This is a great tool for learning what presence feels like. Some of us might not have much experience with being present, so it can be very helpful to have a visceral, felt experience of it to help you to know that you can access it.

As you practice, you might find that some days it only takes two points of focus to become present, and on some days four points may not be enough. On those days you can add another point: focus on the breath.

To add the point of focus on the breath you can either count or mentally repeat a phrase. If you count, you can count as you breathe in for six counts, hold for three counts, breathe out for six counts, hold for three counts, and then repeat. You can shorten or lengthen the counts to whatever amount feels helpful to achieve slow, rhythmic breathing that doesn't feel too forced. If you choose to repeat a phrase, you can mentally say to yourself "breathing in, I'm breathing in" on the inhale, and "breathing out, I'm breathing out" on the exhale.

If you didn't feel present in the previous exercise when you held four points, go ahead and try it with the fifth point of focusing on the breath added in, either with counting the breath, or mentally repeating a phrase.

Try it right now to see if it helps.

If you're still struggling, try adding in a *mudra*, or hand gesture where the tip of the thumb on each hand touches the middle finger of that hand This hand gesture helps to increase focus and patience.

If five points didn't do it for you today, try it again with the mudra added in.

If you tried and you only felt present for one second out of thirty, that's okay. Believe it or not, the practice is still working. Trust that it will get easier, just like anything else. The important thing is not the result, as we've been conditioned to believe, but the experience of practicing.

I recommend practicing the present moment awareness meditation at least once a day. You really only need to do it for thirty to sixty seconds. As you get better at being present, you can add more time. In addition to the full meditation, you can remember to call on the individual pieces of it throughout the day. As you are walking down the street, you could be soaking in the sounds. As you are waiting, you could focus on stillness. When you're hanging out with friends, you could feel your breath and the sensations in your body.

Truly, you can access presence any time and it's very helpful to practice in different situations. It's great to do meditative exercises alone in a controlled environment to strengthen your presence muscle and experiment, but the true practice ground is all throughout our day-to-day existence, in every kind of situation or relationship.

Practice whenever you think of it. Mix it up. Strengthen your will to be present. Notice when you resist. Noticing resistance is a form of presence. Noticing that you haven't been present is a form of presence. The more awareness you cultivate, the more present you are. The more present you are, the more powerful, because all power is here now. Practice every day and then on those days when it feels like the shit is hitting the proverbial fan, you can trust that the power of your presence will be there for you.

## CHAPTER 2 :: KEY POINTS

- Healing is knowing you are already whole.
- Love is healing.
- You are the power and presence of love.
- You can be the space of healing.
- Stillness and presence are healing.
- You can practice presence in any circumstance.
- Presence heals unresolved trauma.
- Unresolved trauma is at the root cause of most mental/emotional/physical symptoms.
- The body will heal itself if you get present with it and love it.

## CHAPTER 2 :: INTEGRATION TIPS

- Bring awareness to the body as many times as you can throughout the day. Notice what's happening in the body. Ask yourself, "What are the sensations I'm feeling in my body right now?"
- Throughout the day, take short mindfulness breaks. Pause, take a breath, close your eyes, feel your body, listen to the sounds. Quantity of time doesn't matter, but quality does. Go all in.
- Notice the times you feel grounded or ungrounded, present or not present. What helps you feel grounded and present? How do you become present and grounded when you're feeling spaced out, upset, or disconnected? Do you hug a tree? Hug your dog? Take a deep breath? Say a prayer? Meditate? Post a note or image somewhere to remind yourself to be grounded and present.

## CHAPTER 2 :: PRACTICUM POSSIBILITIES

**Foundations of your healing practice:** (15 minutes)

Imagine you are creating an inner healing temple in your heart/mind.

What is the quality of this space? Take a moment to dive into it, feel it, explore it. What do you feel when you are there? What are the sensations, sights, sounds?

Journal about anything you discover, even if it is that you didn't discover anything. See if writing about it brings more information or feelings. Take a deep breath of gratitude for all of it.

**Practice releasing trauma:** (as long as it takes)

When you're not feeling triggered, practice using the meditation on Present Moment Awareness given in this chapter to increase your skillfulness in getting present and allowing whatever is to just be.

When you feel triggered by something, practice being compassionate. Stop everything and take a deep breath. Take another. Place a hand on your heart because you love yourself. Tell your body, "I got you, babe. It's okay." Notice what is happening in the body. Cry if you want. Keep breathing. This is radical healing love.

Recognize that every trigger is a healing opportunity. Take a breath of love and gratitude for what has been buried that is now coming up into the light. Take a breath of love and gratitude for your courage to feel it. Take a breath of love and gratitude that now you can let it go.

**Commune with your body:** (10 - 15 minutes)

Lie on the bed or floor and relax with some deep breaths. Bring your awareness into your body. Notice which parts of the body seem to have more energy or sensation or color or warmth. Notice which parts feel numb or dark or painful.

Bring your attention to one of these dark or painful or numb places and ask this part of your body to show you a picture or a feeling of what is going on there. Open yourself to receive any impressions you get. Stay with the body and the sensations. When your mind goes into analyzing or storytelling or wandering, gently come back to the body, the breath and the feelings.

Whether you get a sense of anything or not, thank the body. Thank it for sharing with you. Thank it for always being there for you and for doing its best. And trust that as you practice, eventually you will hear and understand the body's communication with you.

## Observe the cause

consider the quality
of your mind
in this moment
the movement

is it buzzing
from this thought to that

is it soft like
a warm summer breeze
caressing the face
of water laughing
in ripples?

is it gale-force
tearing through
a landscape of crisis?

can you choose
the way the wind blows?

can you
imagine change?

that is the power
for you to harness

the power to change
your mind and choose
your path
to your world

# CHAPTER 3:
# MINDSET AWARENESS

*All healing is at the level of the mind*

## THE POWER OF MINDSET

Mindset is the foundation of everything else in this course. With an empowering mindset anything is possible. Without an empowering mindset, it doesn't matter how good your technique, how savvy your strategy, or how advanced your training.

One of the ways this became clear to me was through the experience of working with different practitioners and teachers. People who trained or worked with me would often assume I had been practicing much longer than I had been. I wondered how I became so proficient so quickly. There seemed to be something that set me apart from other energy workers and teachers that I encountered.

One day I was repeating a Crystal Healing class with my Pranic Healing teacher who had asked if I would assist her. I was tasked with helping set up, keeping the space clear, and making sure there were plenty of snacks and tea for everyone. In exchange, I got to repeat the class.

"How long have you been doing this?" one of my classmates asked. Her eyes twinkled. She smiled at me with a motherly kindness and a confidence that implied she had been doing this for quite some time.

"Um, not very long," I said, wondering what she was getting at, "Maybe a year?"

"I was watching you clear the space earlier and I was wondering what you were doing," Mother Twinkle Eyes said.

"What do you mean?" I asked.

"I see energy clairvoyantly and when you were clearing I saw a brilliant violet light around you, and giant wings behind you."

"Wow, really? Maybe it was an angel helping me?"

"Maybe. That's why I was curious."

"Well, I always invoke for help."

"Were you using any special technique when you were working with the student just now?" she asked.

"Uh, no, I don't think so. Just whatever we were told to practice."

"Hm, interesting."

"Why?"

"Because I saw there was a sphere of light around the two of you, like you had created a protective space to work in."

"Well, if I did, I wasn't aware of it. Maybe my guides did it?"

"Yeah, maybe."

It took me a while to realize that it wasn't an angel or guide. It was me. My mindset had allowed for these energies to come through me. It was a mindset of total trust in what is possible when one is aligned with the light of oneself, because I had already experienced it firsthand.

During the time of the hospital stay that I described in my story in **Chapter 1**, I had the opportunity to have a fully-embodied experience of transmuting pain through a single-pointed focus on the life-force energy of my light and breath. I did this with no training. How? Because my true nature—and yours—is one of knowingness.

Because I tapped into this knowingness, I know beyond a doubt what is possible for each and every one of us. I know that if someone like me—a person who was mentally and physically sick, who was desperate and in pain, who didn't care if they lived or died—has the ability to access the truth of their light, we all have the ability to tap into the truth of our light and the experience of ourselves as all-knowing, all-loving, and all-peaceful.

But what if you don't have the same faith that I have now? That's okay. You can build faith. Faith comes with practicing and demonstrating the efficacy of our choices. We don't need faith to start. I certainly didn't have faith in myself or anything else when I was in that hospital bed. Thankfully, all that's required to tap into our inner knowing and power is the willingness to do it. If we hold a mindset of willingness to let love express through us, we can experience miraculous healing.

## WILLINGNESS

The first step—and sometimes the last—in any healing is to actually be willing to heal. What does it mean to be willing? Willingness means being ready to go for it one hundred percent. It means freely choosing something. It means full and glad participation. It means no holding back. It means being totally interested in doing something. Willingness is intention. It is volition. It is consent. It is an exercise of your power.

With healing work, you must be willing to be committed to total willingness. You don't need to be totally willing right away, but you must at least *be willing* to be willing. You must be willing to allow the healing to happen, willing to let go of what is causing you pain, willing to know the truth of the situation, willing to receive the energy that will support you, willing to trust.

Without your consent, you will not change. Without their consent, other people won't change. Willingness is essential. If you aren't truly willing, you will block whatever it is you think you'd like to experience. You may think you are interested in healing, but you may be unwilling to let go of that which must be released in order for healing to occur.

In order to make a change for the better, we have to be willing to let go of what's not working and willing to embrace what can support us.

This may at first glimpse appear to be simplistic and obvious, but trust me when I say that practicing willingness requires incredible inner strength and determination. That is because there is another powerful mindstate in direct opposition to willingness, and that is resistance.

## RESISTANCE

Resistance is a reaction to change. It's how the unwillingness shows up. For example, if we have attachments to any aspect of the way things are, we might be resistant to changing them. We may feel reluctant because we can't control exactly how the change will manifest in our lives. Sometimes we have intense aversion to uncertainty. We hesitate. We procrastinate. Even positive change, like healing, can trigger uncertainty and reticence.

How many times have you had a good intention to do something and then didn't do it? How many times have you struggled to establish a new healthy habit or release an unhealthy one? How many times have you felt overwhelmed by guilt and shame for not doing what you declared you were willing to do?

I have personally struggled, and continue to struggle, with resistance.

Sometimes I feel like I'm being ripped apart inside by the conflicting energies of desire for change and resistance. It's painful, and yet even this pain is teaching me something. It's teaching me a lot about change and the nature of resistance. It's teaching me about having compassion for the process of change. It's teaching me how to be grateful for all of my experience.

I don't claim to have all the answers, but here are some of the things I practice that help me when I'm experiencing resistance:

- Remember that resistance is a natural response to change.
- Remember that this too shall pass.
- Pause, take deep breaths, and let myself really feel what's happening.
- Allow myself to sit with the resistance mindfully, breathe, and feel it in my body.
- Make a deal with myself that I only have to do the thing I'm resisting for five minutes.
- Listen to what the resistance is saying to me. Notice if it's true.
- See the resistance as a sign that I'm on the path of powerful change.
- Let the resistance be a gift. Be grateful for it.
- Be so spacious that the resistance washes right through me.
- Take an internal warrior stance and blast through the resistance.
- Remind myself that I'm doing this because I love myself.

Note that what is more important than the form of the action is the energy behind it. Is it the energy of compassion, mindfulness, and wisdom, or is it the energy of compulsion, addiction, and powerlessness? If you learn to discern the energy behind the action, you will have a powerful tool that will serve you in all aspects of this work and your life. With this discernment of the underlying energy, you won't be fooled by the forms things appear to take, whether it's resistance or anything else.

We have all experienced resistance in some form and to some degree. Resistance is the energy that comes up in opposition to change. When there is an established pattern, energy is flowing along the pathway of that pattern. That energy flow has momentum, like water flowing down a riverbed. If you'd like to create a new pattern, diverting the existing energy flow to another direction is akin to creating a new riverbed. All the earth that must be carved away for that new pathway to exist is symbolic of the resistance to change.

If you know how powerful resistance is, you can have more compassion for yourself and the struggle to establish new patterns in your life. You can also gain a deeper appreciation for working at the level of the mind, where the energy is easier to shift than it is in the denser energy of the physical world.

## THE CAUSAL LEVEL

The mental level is also known as the causal level because all things that manifest spring from a thought. First we have an idea, then we feel an emotional response, and then there is a corresponding physical response. Ideas are the cause of the effects we see in the world of form. Everything you see in the human-made world began as an idea in someone's imagination. That's why it's so important to fully grasp the power of your mind and how to work with it effectively. Your thoughts create reality.

That is also why we are beginning our exploration of Lightworker Training with consciousness tools and not energy work. Energy work deals with symptoms, correcting things that have already manifested in the energy field or physical body. Consciousness work, on the other hand, involves cultivating awareness to make corrections at the causal level of mind. Energy work tools are helpful to clean up the effects of what has already been created from past thoughts, but conscious awareness is essential to creating new mindsets, choosing new thoughts and manifesting new patterns.

If you think about it, all healing happens at the level of the mind, because true healing is creating a shift at the root cause, not just treating symptoms. If everything that manifests proceeds from a thought, the mind is the only thing there is to heal.

## RECOGNIZING THE SPLIT MIND

If you'd like to learn more about your mind and healing it, a great place to start is by observing your thoughts. The more you observe, the more you will discover that your mind appears to be split between helpful thoughts which create more clarity and peace, and unhelpful thoughts which create more confusion and conflict.

The concept of the split mind is incredibly helpful to understand, not only for this work, but for navigating everyday life with more grace and freedom from suffering. (In truth, the separation—or split—that we experience never happened, but we *believe* it did.)

In the split mind, there is identification as finite body, control, personality, ego, and separation on one side, and identification as infinite, spirit, power, love, oneness, and unity consciousness on the other. When you can recognize that you are vacillating between these two mindstates, you start to perceive that one is fearful, and prone to thoughts of lack, attack, limitation, and judgment, and the other is calm, peaceful, empowered, and loving.

As you become more aware of your thoughts and their effects on your emotional state, you will start to notice that when you choose to activate loving thoughts you will feel and see more beneficial effects, and when you choose to activate unloving thoughts you will experience more upsetting effects. The more you recognize the effects of your causal thoughts, the more quickly you will learn with which mindstate you prefer to create. The thoughts that trigger upsetting feelings show us very clearly when we're identified with separation, lack, attack, and limitation.

It is helpful to know that the more stark the contrast between peace and upset, the easier the discernment of the underlying energy and, hence, the clearer your choices become. The more upset you are, the greater the opportunity to experience deep healing. An example that comes to mind of how I personally took advantage of a tremendously upsetting situation and used it for profound healing is the following story.

## MAKING THE CHOICE

Back in February 2007, two weeks after the experience of being immersed in the light of my being, I was being prepped to leave the hospital. I didn't feel ready to leave, but the team of doctors working with me had decided that because hospitals are the most likely place to get a MRSA infection, it was important to discharge me as soon as possible to prevent my weakened immune system from being bombarded with yet another superbug infestation. My left eye was still very swollen from the trauma of inflammation and surgery and had been sewn shut to prevent it from popping out of my head. I had an IV catheter line inserted in my left arm that ran to a large vein near my heart. I was taught how to hook it up to tubes and syringes and pumps. I didn't feel prepared to handle such an important job. I was scared I would mess something up. I was afraid I would create more suffering for myself. Even the comfort of being taken care of in the hospital was over. I was on my own.

At that point, even getting out of bed felt heroic. I felt so weak and helpless. My whole life I had identified as a badass, a dancer, a bicyclist, a yogi, and now I could barely bathe myself without crying. The gigs I had at the time, cutting hair, making jewelry, creating window displays, helping people organize and style their homes, all depended on my sight, and now I was facing the possibility that I might lose one of my eyes, or at least vision in it. Before the illness, I saw myself as a relatively healthy, strong, and attractive woman who was totally capable of taking care of herself and anyone else. Afterward, I was struggling to take care of my body's basic needs, I was exhausted by dealing with people's responses to the disfigurement of my face, and was feeling a deep loss of my identity and purpose.

During the two and a half months I spent at home recovering and hooking myself up to IVs five times a day, I felt the fear of my identity being stripped away. Just my body and I were left. Every day I struggled with being overwhelmed by the smallest tasks, being constantly nauseous from the antibiotics, constantly in pain despite the drugs, and worried that I would contract some secondary disease from all my intestinal flora being wiped out. When I was in the hospital I was too close to death to worry about life, but now that I was at home, I was in a constant war with my fear-based thoughts. It was exhausting. The only relief I had from worrying was sleep. I slept a lot.

When I was conscious, the tiniest tasks felt overwhelming, but those tasks taught me about the power of my will. I figured if I could get through that period, I could get through anything. To do that, I would have to surrender to life completely. I would have to focus my mind, like I focused on the light in the center of my being. I had to let go of my old way of being in the world. I couldn't go back. I couldn't power through anymore. I had to find a new way. A way not only to manage and cope, but a way to transcend suffering. A way to feel empowered despite whatever might be happening with my body, a way to feel lovable despite my inability to do things for others, and a way to feel beautiful despite what my physical appearance was. It was a path back to my true self, back to the light I had experienced and then so quickly forgotten.

In contemplative states, I began to see clearly the branched path and two ways set before me: the path of ego identification and suffering on the one hand, and the path of spirit identification and freedom on the other. I chose the path of freedom and I continued to choose it every day. Every time I started slipping back into the darkness of my fear, I had an opportunity to choose again. And again.

I had no idea how far-reaching the implications of those choices would be. At the time, it was simply a matter of survival. It started with simple, daily actions of choosing peaceful thoughts instead of upsetting ones. I didn't realize it until much later, but with those choices, I had entered the path of training myself to be a lightworker, an alchemist, a spiritual warrior. I was on the path of mind mastery.

## HEALING AT THE LEVEL OF THE MIND

Throughout this course we will work together toward mind mastery and return to the concept of the two paths, or the two mind states. We will cultivate awareness of what mind state we are in at a given time and the importance of recognizing the choices available to us in the moment. If we are in doubt, fear, or feeling stuck, we are identified with separation and our egos. If we'd like to be in a more peaceful state, we can shift to the lightness and peace of unity consciousness. In this book we will explore several tools for doing exactly that. The key, as always, is to be willing. If you are willing to change your mind, you can change your reality.

In our day-to-day lives, we are vacillating between the two parts of our split minds: the one aligned with unity consciousness and the one aligned with belief in separation. One is sane and the other is not. One is only interested in peace, and one is more interested in its own judgments and opinions than in peace, even if it means feeling lost, scared, victimized, ashamed, guilty, attacked, and upset. You are either in one mindset or the other, because being in one requires complete relinquishment of the other. Even a tiny upset will require the total loss of your peace.

Remember, in truth, that the separation never occurred. We only think it did. It is merely a mistaken belief in something impossible. Once you understand this, you can accomplish anything because you understand that nothing need be done. All that is required to have a miraculous healing is to relinquish attachment to insane thoughts of separation and choose to be at peace in the oneness. Luckily, this teaching is very simple and clear, because in practice it requires constant vigilance, great willingness, and determination to stay on the path of love.

Steering clear of the many traps and pitfalls of our individual and collective ego beliefs can feel like quite the balancing act sometimes. Like meditation, or any form of non-doing, the practice of being only in your sane and loving mind can be more easily comprehended than accomplished, but it does get easier the more it is practiced. Releasing attachments can sometimes trigger resistance and fear because we have become so identified as our ego/body/separate selves that we don't know who or what we'd be if we let go. That's okay. It's all part of the process of remembering and returning to our true nature.

The wonderful thing about the practice of choosing to live in your sane mind is that with it you can make a top-down shift in your energy field. Working with the relatively easy-to-shift mental energy at the causal level will filter down into the denser levels of the emotional, etheric, and physical bodies where the effects are felt. On the other hand, if you address physical and emotional symptoms, but you don't correct the problem at the level of the mind, the emotional and physical effects will return. How many times have we despaired at the seemingly endless repetition of painful patterns because we didn't understand the root cause? Now we are learning that the root cause is always somewhere in the mind.

Over time, the energies which started at the causal level of the mind become what we see concretized in the world of physical forms. Recognize that what you see now is the concretization of past thoughts. What you will see in the future depends on the thoughts you choose now.

It is helpful to remember that the world we see is not only a reflection of our individual minds, but also an expression of the collective consciousness, all of our minds creating together. We are seeing the results of our past collective thoughts and beliefs energized by the power of our collective mind. That is a lot of energy and it can sometimes feel disheartening to choose something different than the dominant paradigm, but because all minds are joined at the level of unified consciousness, we can and are affecting everything in the collective with our thoughts.

Just like our thoughts ripple down into the world of form, they also ripple out into the collective mind. They pick up momentum and power by combining with other like-minded energies and create even more impact. Furthermore, the thoughts we think in alignment with our true nature are *eternal*, rippling out and creating forever.

Our thoughts are powerful, because our minds are powerful. Our minds are amazing computers that will run any program that is installed. Those mental programs, beliefs, and ideas are how we are creating our lives on the causal level, but where do those ideas originate? Are they even ours?

## WHO DOES THAT THOUGHT BELONG TO?

If you have been paying attention to your thoughts, you may have discovered that some of them are beliefs that come from your upbringing or social conditioning or have some other discernible source. But did you know that you can also pick up thoughts from random people?

Have you ever observed your thoughts and had an awareness that some of them didn't feel like you, even though they were in your mind? Maybe out of the blue you started worrying about taking care of babies when you don't even have a baby, or got angry in traffic when you really aren't the road-rage type. These thoughts most likely aren't yours.

Because you share one mind with everyone in the collective, you can think other people's thoughts. Everyone does this. Yes, even you. We are all hard-wired this way, but unfortunately, we're not taught this, so we assume that every thought we have is ours when it most likely isn't. As a matter of fact, *most* of the thoughts you have aren't yours. Pretty wild, right?

**We are all way more psychic than we think we are.**

I invite you to try this: next time you get a thought or a feeling, ask your-self, "Who does that belong to?" and notice if the thought or feeling shifts. Maybe you get an awareness that it belongs to someone else. Maybe you realize that you made it up after all.

I once did a week-long experiment wherein I asked the question, "Who does that belong to?" for every thought and feeling I was aware of and I also added, "Return to sender with consciousness attached," if it seemed like a painful or sticky one. Of course I didn't catch all—or even most—of my thoughts and feelings, because I wasn't present enough to do that, but even with the percentage that I did catch I noticed a enormous difference.

After clearing thousands of thoughts from other people every day, I started to feel a lot more spacious and peaceful, even meditative. There was so much space in my mind that I started to be aware of when thoughts would drift in. I felt more grounded, present, and more myself. It was pretty amaz-ing, really.

So I kept that practice in my awareness, not doing it so intensely, but hav-ing an intention to be conscious of it. After a while, I started to notice I would go for whole minutes without having a single thought. As time went on, those periods of time got steadily longer and appeared more frequently. I would sometimes catch myself not thinking and I would be shocked. Bear in mind, my previous default state was over-thinking everything. I used to have terrible insomnia, anxiety, and panic attacks because my mind was in overdrive all the time, so even having one brief moment's peace with no intruding thoughts was truly a miracle. Now, with willingness and practice, I experience this miraculous state of mind more often than not. You can, too. Just start with the question, "Who does that belong to?" and see what happens.

Asking the question "Who does that belong to?" is a fun mental technique for creating space and uncluttering your mind. Another way is through the Present Moment Awareness meditation from **Chapter 2: Foundations of Healing**. There are many others, but remember: although extremely helpful for beginners, techniques are optional. All that is truly required is your willingness to release the clutter and let your mind be clear. You learn how to do it in your practice of it.

Why focus on clearing your mind? Because the less mental clutter there is, the easier it will be to focus on what you'd like to, instead of all the distractions that draw your energy. It will also be easier to hear the guidance of your inner teacher and easier to stay focused on the present moment where all the power is.

## ALL THOUGHTS ARE CREATIVE

All of our thoughts are creative, even the painful, unloving ones. All thoughts are creating form at some level. The world we see is a creative projection of the past thoughts of the collective consciousness. If we would like to change something in the world of form, the most potent and practical thing we can do is change our minds about it. This Michael Beckwith quote sums it up nicely:

*"When you believe more in what you don't see than what you do see, you will see what you don't see and you won't see what you do see."*

Because the level of the mind is the causal level, we must make a shift there to change the patterns that occur in our emotions, our bodies, our lives, and our world. That is why working at the level of the symptom, or effect, is not enough to create lasting change and permanent healing. When we work at the causal level, we can create a new mental program, which is like a computer program or blueprint. Your mind is the computer and your thoughts are the programs. You are the user. You get to decide what your computer is going to do for you.

Do you ever wonder what kinds of mental programs you're running? Take a moment to think about your beliefs and the stories you tell yourself. Think about the meaning you assign to things and events. Are these mental programs helpful? Are you creating from a mindset of love or a mindset of fear?

The process of re-programming is really very simple and straightforward, but it requires the determination and willingness of consistent practice. The practice consists of being aware of your thoughts, choosing to keep the ones you like, and deleting the rest. You don't have to figure out how to do it. You just choose it. The "how" actually shows up after the choice to do it.

It's helpful to note that the separate-self or ego loves to keep you confused about trying to figure things out, because that is one of the ways it ensures its place of prominence in your mind. I like to remind myself that the aspect of my mind that is trying to figure something out will never be able to, because the answer is beyond what the separate-self can fathom. Not only that, but the mind that is capable of figuring it out would never be trying to figure it out, because it already knows.

It's like that famous quote attributed to Einstein that you can never solve a problem with the mind that created it.

To tap into the creative power of our minds, we must release our belief that we need to know how first. We must make a quantum leap from separation thinking into the unified mind where all things are known. As we take this leap, we must trust that in the moment we choose it, we will create, receive, or teach ourselves the tools we most need to learn.

## ON KEEPING IT LIGHT

One of the fastest methods for clearing the energy of upset is laughter. It is healing to laugh at our egoic blunders. When you get upset at your mistakes, you give your power away to the thing that is upsetting you, but at any time you can reclaim your power to be at peace. The truth is, no one or thing has the power to make you think or feel a certain way. When you laugh at mishaps, you reaffirm they are laughable and have no power to make you upset.

When you understand that separation is an illusion and ego personality constructs are a fabrication that exist only in the mind, you can afford to take them way less seriously. When you realize that the separate-self/ego is an insane belief system that interprets everything it perceives in a completely backwards, upside-down way, you can laugh at its clumsy attempts to gain the light of your attention. What is ridiculous must clearly be laughable and not taken seriously.

I understand how laughing at perceived mistakes may be challenging at first. Because I was punished as a child for making innocent mistakes, I developed a tremendous aversion to making them. When mistakes inevitably happened, I would panic and have emotional meltdowns or go into denial of being wrong, adamantly arguing my case to prove my innocence. Even after I recognized that those upsets were caused by old trauma getting triggered, I would still get upset. Oftentimes I was upset because I was upset. The thing that eventually saved me from this insanity was my sense of humor. From talking to friends who could take a light-hearted perspective on their mistakes and watching or listening to a lot of comedy that exploited such follies, I learned that the things that upset me the most were also ripe for transmuting into comedic gold. I learned that if I could laugh at my mistakes they would cease to have the power to take away my peace.

Something else that has lightened my emotional load is knowing that in truth, *there are no mistakes*. Every single experience has within it a jewel of wisdom for us if we are willing to receive it. Spirit can take anything and turn it into gold, just as the ego can take anything and turn it into suffering.

This light-hearted approach is essential for our own peace of mind, healing, and resiliency, especially at this time in the history of our collective evolution, when there is more coming up for healing than ever before. As we shift the ancient patterns of separation, integrate existing shadow elements, and awaken to our true nature, it's easy to feel overwhelmed.

Keeping a lightness in your mind and your heart will support you in all aspects of your life, give you alternative perspectives to seemingly hopeless situations, and keep you from falling into energy-draining patterns of despair.

It is a radical act of loving kindness to laugh in the face of darkness. It is a radical act of power to smile at a perceived enemy. It is a radical act of compassion to chuckle at the missteps and foibles of the ego.

As we go through the practices in this text, there will no doubt be some pretty heavy energy that gets stirred up. The most powerful way to transmute it is not to match it in frequency, but to stay up in a high vibration of lightness, allowing grace and ease to flow through you. Remember, the light doesn't think to itself, "I don't know. This space is really, really dark. What if I can't shine in all this darkness?" It simply shines and the darkness is gone.

## CHAPTER 3 :: KEY POINTS

• Mindset is the foundation of all practices.
• The most empowering mindset is one of willingness.
• Resistance is a natural response to change.
• Causation occurs at the mental level.
• The level of form is the level of effect.
• To create lasting change, one must work at the level of cause.
• Our minds appear to be split between the natural mind and the artificial personality constructs of the ego.
• The split never actually happened, but the split mind concept can be a helpful tool for discerning which mind state we are identified with.
• We can choose which mindstate we would like to experience.
• All thoughts create form at some level.
• We are all way more psychic than we think we are.

• There are no mistakes, there is only learning.

## CHAPTER 3 :: INTEGRATION TIPS

• Throughout the day, check in to see what's happening in your mind. What mindstate are you in? What are you thinking? Simply observe.
• If there is a time when you feel upset, take a breath and imagine you are making a quantum leap into another mindstate. Release the "how" and embrace the "what."
• When you get angry, see if you can be grateful. See if you can appreciate your passion. See if you can discern what is really upsetting you. See if you can laugh at yourself. See if you can be compassionate with yourself.
• Imagine everything that comes into your mind is just an interesting point of view. You might even say to yourself, "Interesting point of view. I have that point of view." Notice if you have resistance to being open to an interesting point of view.

## CHAPTER 3 :: PRACTICUM POSSIBILITIES

**Change your mind, change the world:** (5 - 10 minutes)

Can you remember a time when you changed your mind about something and it shifted the dynamic in the world of form? Some examples include:

• You stopped judging a friend/partner/co-worker/your body and in some way it changed the relationship you had with it.
• You stopped resisting doing homework/laundry/dishes and it became more enjoyable.
• You changed a story in your mind about being victimized/broke/attacked/unloved and you felt more empowered.
• You decided you were unwilling to settle for the same old painful patterns and you noticed a shift without "doing" anything.
• When something potentially upsetting occurred, you chose to let it go, or even laugh, instead of being upset and it totally transformed your experience of the situation.

What are some examples from your life or things you've witnessed in others? Take a moment to reflect, remember what it felt like, and make notes in your journal if you like. See if you'd like to take this awareness and apply it consciously moving forward.

**Take a mental inventory:** (as long as you like, whenever you like)

For this exercise, take some time to journal about what you observe in your mind. The goal is to become more aware of negative mental programs. Here are some ideas to get you started:

• What are some of the repetitive thoughts you have? (For example: *I wish I were better. I don't have enough money. I can't. I have to do this. If only it were different.*)
• What are the stories you tell? (*I never do that. This always happens. I'm not good at math.*)
• Where does your mind tend to go? Replaying the past, fixating on the future? Obsessing about other people? Worrying about what to do? (*If only I wouldn't have done that. What if it doesn't work? What if she doesn't like me?*)
• What meaning do you attribute to things? (*If you cared you would do it. It's because I'm such a loser. It's fate.*)

Notice what is coming up. Are these programs and patterns helpful? Could they use an upgrade?

Often when we first start observing our minds we don't have much, if any, awareness of what our thoughts even are. That is perfectly normal and that is why we practice. We typically don't catch thoughts until they trigger an emotional response. Our emotions are showing us what thoughts we are thinking, so every emotion is helpful.

Don't worry if what you're thinking isn't clear yet. Imagine that this exercise is an intention to observe your thoughts and gain that clarity so that you can have more choice over the programming in your mental computer.

You can even imagine deleting the programs you don't like. Your imagination, intention, and willingness have great power.

**Shadow inventory, part 2:** (as long as you like)

Write in your journal a list of all the shadow aspects of your mind that you're aware of in this moment. All of the unloving thought patterns, the things you judge as wrong, the things that cause you pain. Write down your perceived limitations and blocks. Write about the aspects of yourself or your life with which you struggle. Ask your shadow what it would like to share.

Write about the things that drive you nuts about other people in your life or in the world. Do you hate that someone is judgmental or lazy? See if you can recognize a disowned part of yourself that wants to criticize or shirk responsibility. Do you hate greedy, selfish jerks? See if there is a part of you that wishes it could do that, too. Feel into your own inner conflict.

Notice how much energy of resistance there is to acknowledging your shadow. Notice if there is fear. Notice if you can be with it. Notice if you want to run away. If a lot of emotion arises, let it flow and wash out. Take time to process. If there is something you are ready to let go of, practice being willing to release it without any attachment to the outcome.

When you feel complete with your exploration, take a few deep breaths of love and gratitude for all the aspects of yourself, drink some water and ground down by touching the earth with your body or imagining touching it in your mind. Remind yourself that the Earth supports all of her children whether we judge them as good or bad. See if you can take a page from nature and be willing to shine the light of your love on all aspects of yourself.

If you'd like additional clearing support, take a salt bath or shower. If a lot comes up to process, be sure to take some time to rest.

### What you know

from the vast sea of being
you arise and return

the mother of all
awaits you within

come home to this moment
immersed in sensations

feelings illuminate
what cries for healing
and what lies below

you can read in the ripples
the turn of the breeze
and anticipate tides
of energy flows

ebbing emotions
wash through receding

all that is needed
you already know

# CHAPTER 4:
# DEVELOPMENT OF INTUITION

*The only thing that keeps you from your knowing is denial of it*

## INTUITION

Intuition is often thought of as a special gift or supernatural skill that only select people have. It's not. Whether you call it gut feeling, instinct, sixth sense, clairsentience, or the voice of spirit, we all have access to intuitive abilities. It's actually more natural to follow your intuition than to not.

The reason more people don't avail themselves of this natural ability is simple: we have been conditioned to shut down our inner guidance system and to deny that aspect of our knowingness. The good news is that because intuition is an inborn aspect of your ability to sense and know, if you are willing to reactivate it, you are guaranteed to be successful.

Intuitive information comes from a multitude of sources, but it can be helpful to break them into two main categories: physical and mental.

The following examples represent a few of the ways physical intuition manifests:

- You feel when someone is in a bad mood.
- There's a sense that something is "off."
- You notice the energy in a place feels weird.
- You can sense someone staring at you.
- You can tell a situation is dangerous.
- You feel sudden fear/chills/hair standing on end.

These are all examples of primal brain/body level awareness designed for the survival of the individual organism.

Notice how those physical survival messages differ from the following examples of the mental form of intuition:

- You think about a friend right before they call you.
- You think about an old movie right before you see a clip from it posted on social media.
- You think about a song, then walk into a coffee shop and hear it playing.
- You decide to wear a red shirt to the gym and almost everyone else is wearing a red shirt.
- You decide to take a different route and run into someone who's been thinking of you.

These types of synchronous events are due to our individual minds being part of the shared mind of the larger organism.

Basically, intuitive information is either coming from the individual subconscious mind of your body or from the collective mind that we share. Whether the source is physical or mental, it is helpful to be open to receiving it. By listening to and following your intuitive guidance, you can save vast amounts of time and energy spent in frustration. Being in tune with your intuition could even save your life.

## THE LANGUAGE OF INTUITION

The first step in following intuitive guidance is to have an awareness of the diverse ways in which it is sharing information with you. Intuition speaks in sensations, thoughts, feelings, emotions and knowingness.

You may have had experiences of, or know of some of these ways that intuitive information shows up:

- **A sensation**: your hairs stand on end, you have butterflies in your stomach, you feel dizzy or nauseous, or chills run up your back.
- **A thought**: you think to yourself, "This doesn't feel right," or, "I should go this way instead," and you don't have a logical explanation of why you would think that.
- **An emotion**: you suddenly feel unexplained fear, anxiety, dread, joy, or sadness that doesn't feel like it's yours.
- **A feeling**: you feel the energy of heaviness or lightness, a sense of time slowing down, the room moving, or sudden air pressure changes.
- **A knowingness**: you get instant knowledge of something or the whole story of something without being able to explain how you know.
- **A visual**: you see something out of the corner of your eye, colors/light/darkness around people or things, a picture in your mind, or a flash of a visual image.

These different streams of information come from the different intelligences: body intelligence, mental intelligence, emotional intelligence, sentient intelligence, and collective intelligence. In the phenomena listed above, there are examples of positive and negative messages. The energy of the impression you receive is more relevant than the form it takes. For example, receiving the information of a highly charged positive energy is more relevant than whether it came in the form of a sensation in your body or a knowingness.

Whenever there is a question, or a questionable situation, there are many possible responses, but they all fit into one of three simple categories: positive, negative, or neutral. If you can discern whether the information you receive from an intelligent source is positive, negative, or neutral, you have the ability to follow intuitive guidance.

For example, let's say a friend asks if you'd like to go on a river outing with them this weekend. For no apparent reason, you feel heavy and filled with dread at the prospect. That would indicate a negative response. That negative response is showing you in a very clear way the most helpful course of action to take. Perhaps your body is telling you that what it would really like is some time spent alone, resting. Perhaps there is something else that becomes clear later on, like the weather takes a turn for the worse, or you get an amazing opportunity that you would have missed if you were out of town. Who knows? You do. Part of your consciousness knows. Trust it.

What about if you're asked to do something and you suddenly feel light, expanded, and filled with joy? Do you think that might be a sign that there's positive energy there for you?

## KEEP IT SIMPLE, SWEETHEART

The important thing to remember about intuition is to keep it simple. You don't have to figure out why something does or doesn't feel right. As a matter of fact, over-thinking things can create confusion at best and severely compromise personal safety at worst.

Most of us have been taught as children in school that if we can't explain something or prove it to be true, it isn't valid. I'm here to bust that belief and tell you that your intuition is a completely valid and powerful tool that will support you in ways that nothing else can. Trust it.

Here is a simple guide to interpreting the language of intuition:

- If it feels negative, it's a NO.
- If it feels positive, it's a YES.
- If it feels neutral, more information is required before making a decision.

Such clarity and simplicity are tremendously helpful, because the practice of following this clear guidance is surprisingly tricky. That's due to a little thing called denial.

## DENIAL

Denial is resistance to knowing the truth. Denial is the enemy of intuition. Denial is suddenly being afraid that someone is going to hurt you and saying to yourself, "But he seems like such a nice guy, why would I imagine such a horrible thing? There must be something wrong with me. I don't want to offend anyone. What if I'm wrong?"

Denial is not wanting to go to the river with your friend but saying to yourself, "That's crazy, of course I should go. Summer only comes once a year. What if I don't get another chance to go swimming?"

Intuition will never argue a case like denial will, so there's a clue right there that it's not your intuition convincing you that you should do a, b, and c because x, y, and z. Intuition just says, "yes, do that" or "no, don't do that" very clearly and concisely.

But because intuitive information comes from intelligence systems that operate outside of our typical awareness, there is a tendency to discount that information or judge it as not making sense. Just because it doesn't seem to make sense to our conscious minds doesn't mean that it doesn't make sense. Remember, the mental processes we are able to be aware of at this time are a very tiny percentage of overall brain activity.

It is currently believed that we are consciously aware of only about 5% of our mental processes and the remaining 95% are unfolding subconsciously. Wouldn't it behoove us to pay attention when the 95% is speaking to us? And that's just the physical brain. We also receive information through the infinite mind we share with all of creation.

If we remember that much of what our minds are picking up on is outside of our conscious, individual thoughts, we may be more willing to give our intuition the credence it deserves and not deny the information when it comes.

Another reason denial is so tempting is because possible danger, confrontation, or even saying "no" is frightening for many of us. When faced with this fear, our minds sometimes go into a state of denial, making up reasons why this can't be happening, contrary to what our senses are clearly showing us.

We often think we are being crazy by paying heed to our feelings, but are we? These so-called illogical feelings are based in complex information-gathering and intelligence systems that are far beyond what our typical conscious awareness can process. If we acknowledge that these vastly complex systems are highly intelligent and specifically designed for our survival and well-being, we might recognize that we'd be crazy not to listen to our intuition.

## RELEASING DENIAL

The primary requirement for clearing the blocks of denial is the same as clearing anything: willingness. That is why learning about things like intuition, denial, consciousness, and fear response is helpful. Not because that information is required to clear denial, but because with greater understanding comes greater willingness to act.

The more you understand the power of the subconscious information-gathering system, the more you may be willing to listen to what it is communicating. Denial is a deeply entrenched thought system or habit, so to defeat it we must exercise willingness to know the truth, willingness to listen to our guidance, and willingness to trust it when it comes.

In my practice of lightwork, I rely heavily on scanning energies and listening to my intuition. When I first started using these tools, I would frequently doubt or deny what I was seeing or scanning. I would pick up on something and think, "What if that's not right? What if I'm just making this up?" or sometimes even, "That can't be right."

It took practice, praying for help, acting on guidance, and getting positive feedback to develop the trust I have in my scanning ability today.

Part of the reason I like to encourage students to practice intuitive work with other willing participants is because through those interactions they can receive the valuable feedback and affirmation that is so helpful in building trust in their intuition and confidence in their skills.

Since we've been conditioned to deny what we know, it takes a leap of faith to trust our empathic and psychic knowing. My hope is that by sharing this with you, you will come to understand that denial is normal. Not trusting your intuition at first is normal. And trusting yourself gets easier with practice.

If you know denial will block your intuition, you can be aware of it when it arises and choose something else. If you are having trouble getting an accurate read on something, one of the first things to do is to clear any denial to knowing the truth. You can say, "I am willing to clear all my resistance and denial about this now and know the truth."

We'll look more at clearing attachments and blocks in Part 2, but for now, just be aware that all that is required to receive the truth of what your intuition is showing you is the willingness to let go of the denial of it.

## DEVELOPMENT OF TRUST

How many times have we known something, denied it, later said, "I knew it!" and then judged ourselves for not listening to our intuition? How many times have we presented this evidence against ourselves as proof of being untrustworthy? How many times have we punished ourselves with unloving thoughts? How many times have we despaired at the seemingly hopeless repetition of painful patterns like this? But, what if we're not the ones who are untrustworthy?

Remember the split mind concept? In the split mind, we vacillate between the knowingness of our true selves and the thoughts of the ego belief system. The ego is always untrustworthy, because it's deluded. The ego will always be in denial of the truth, because the truth would destroy it. If you haven't yet discerned the difference between the ego's voice and yours, you may think it sounds like you, but it doesn't. It seems like the ego's thoughts are your thoughts, but they are not.

Your true thoughts are sane. Your true thoughts are loving. Even when they are illuminating something you might not want to look at, your true thoughts will be calm and helpful. The ego's thoughts are neurotic and delusional. Only the ego would think that denying the truth could make a lie be true. If you know that the ego operates like this, it is much easier to have compassion for yourself when you follow the ego's delusions instead of your true guidance. In the madness, you can recognize the untrustworthy nature of the false-self and you can remember that your true guidance is still trustworthy and will never let you down.

Your true guidance stems from a natural connection to your body and the oneness of all life. When you are identifying as your true self and not the personality construct of the ego, you will naturally be connected with the consciousness that creates and sustains the universe. That universal love/light/information is flowing through everything all the time. It is completely trustworthy because it is all-knowing and it has everyone's best interests in mind. It is an infinite source of intelligence that is yours to receive.

I can tell you this and you can understand it intellectually and that's great, but that's not how you build trust in yourself. You have to have a lived experience of it. Our spiritual development and learning happens in the demonstration of knowledge through our actions. Through our actions, we teach ourselves and others the efficacy of our choices. If we choose to follow the ego, we will experience the pain of separation. If we choose to follow our inner teacher, we will experience our true nature, which is pleasure and connection.

Every time we choose a causal thought and experience its effects, we learn. Every time we choose to follow our intuition or inner guidance, we demonstrate our trustworthiness. Trust is like a muscle: every time you use it, it gets stronger. Little by little, you will build unshakable trust in your true self and your ability to follow your guidance. You will be a living, breathing embodiment of the peace that results from deep trust and faith.

## DISCERNMENT

The more open you are to information flowing through your mind and body, the more opportunity you will have to practice discernment. When something comes into your awareness, it is extremely helpful to discern if it is guidance meant for you, or if it is some other kind of information floating in the ether that you are picking up on.

Remember, you are more psychic than you know and you are able to receive other people's thoughts and feelings in your mind/body. Therefore, not everything that comes into your awareness is necessarily meant for you to act upon. To gain clarity, it is helpful to ask questions.

**Questions for mental discernment:**

- Who does this (thought/feeling) belong to? Is it mine or someone else's?
- Is this for me? Is this for me to do? Is this for me to do *now*?
- Is this guidance from my higher self (or my body) or is this my ego?

When it comes to mental discernment and making decisions, for example, about whether or not you are feeling called to follow a new career path in life, it is helpful to go through the list of questions above to make sure it is truly your inner teacher speaking to you and not just some random thoughts floating around on the psychic airwaves.

If you're thinking about a new career or moving cross-country, those are the kinds of situations in which you have time to deliberate and your body is safe, but in situations when you suddenly get a bad feeling about someone or something that affects your physical safety, it is crucial to act quickly.

**If you are in a situation where you suddenly get a gut feeling about your body being unsafe, act on your feelings immediately.**

Sudden gut feelings of fear are most likely coming directly from your brain/body's subconscious information processing centers and those impulses are designed for your body's survival. There's a chance that it's not your body's alarm system and everything is okay, but that is a chance you don't want to take. Trust me. It is far better to cross the street, leave the party, run away, or head to a safer place than run the risk of being involved in a dangerous situation because you didn't want to appear crazy or offend someone. Your safety is more important than someone's feelings.

As for the other kind of intuitive guidance—the mental kind—rather than act quickly, it is typically more beneficial to wait and use some discernment.

Looking back on your life, can you pinpoint times that you used good discernment? What did it feel like to get an intuitive sense of something and follow through? What did it feel like to trust yourself? I invite you to acknowledge this because we typically focus more on the times we *didn't* listen to our intuition.

If you are focused on the times you were totally wrapped up in denial and not listening to your inner guidance, I invite you to try an experiment: see if you can look back at these experiences and view them through a perspective of compassion for yourself. See if you can chalk it all up to building your wisdom. After all, knowing what not to do is just as valuable as knowing what to do.

And for the next time you're not sure what to do, I invite you to remember this:

• You already know what *not* to do based on past experience. You know it is not helpful to go into denial or ego identification.
• You know that you can tap into your inner guidance system by being willing to be open and listen.
• You know how to be calm and wait for the truth of your clear guidance to become evident.
• You know how to act when your guidance becomes clear.

That is the truth. You may not have a lot of practice with any one of these things, but you do know how to do them because they are all a part of your true nature.

## GET OUT OF YOUR HEAD AND INTO YOUR HEART

One of the keys to successfully connecting with your intuitive nature is to stop thinking about it. Intuition isn't thinking, it's knowing. Would you rather think you know something or know you know it?

The thing is, with thinking, you can usually explain why you think what you do, but with intuitive knowing, you can't explain it, you just know it. Not being able to explain something collides with our social conditioning. We are taught that we must be able to demonstrate in a logical, linear way how we got from point A to point B. Unfortunately, this is not the way the truth works.

**The truth doesn't care if you can prove it or not.**

Much of the true information we receive is non-linear, non-logical, and subconscious. But just because we can't explain it with the tiny percentage of brain power available to compute things on the conscious level, that doesn't mean it's not valid.

What if the truth is not something that you learn, but rather something that is remembered that you already know? What if your natural way of being is in alignment with truth? That you are hard-wired to know it, to feel it? So that when you encounter it, it is as though something is resonating within you, like a tuning fork vibrating with the frequency of truth?

This intuitive way of accessing information is more easily tapped into through the feeling power of our hearts rather than the computing power of our brains.

## THE POWER OF YOUR HEART

Did you know the electromagnetic field of your heart is more powerful than the field of your brain? The heart's electrical field is about 60 times greater in amplitude than that of the brain and the magnetic field is about *5000 times* stronger.

The heart is better equipped to feel, resonate with, and discern the various frequencies of information in the collective field than the brain is. It's through the energetic powerhouse of the heart that we feel into what is true for us in the moment.

Many of us spend the majority of our days in our heads, thinking about things, talking to ourselves, ruminating, worrying, contemplating, and strategizing. The technological devices we are surrounded with and the information streaming through them is an extension of our mental energy. All the information we are taking in through our eyes and ears is continually being processed mentally.

Our brains filter so much information, so many messages, thoughts, and beliefs, it can sometimes be difficult to discern what our truth is in all of it. How many times have we tried to use our brain power to figure out what the truth is? How many times have we tried to look it up, to find it somewhere "out there," and to prove it to ourselves? How exhausting is that? What if we could simply open to know it?

When we open to the intelligence of our heart-minds, we open to ways of direct knowing. We open to feeling the truth resonate within us. I like to think of it as getting out of our heads and into our hearts. The way I shift into that state of being is to pause, take a deep breath, and imagine I am dropping all that mental energy from my head space down into my heart space. As I continue to breathe, I imagine my heart opening and expanding. As I do this, I feel my body relax. I feel more grounded and centered. I feel like I am accessing a deep wisdom of my body, nature, and spirit that is beyond my intellect, my understanding, and my explanation, and yet is somehow within my knowing. In this state I feel calm, strong, resilient, and able to respond to whatever arises with total capability. This leads me to feel grateful and the gratitude strengthens the feeling even more.

Try it. Take a moment now to close your eyes, take a deep breath and imagine you are dropping your mental energy into your heart. Notice how it feels.

..........................................

Did it feel more spacious? Perhaps even 60 to 5,000 times more spacious?

Spending time in your heart space and feeling into what is true there is a practice. It is a process not of creating something new, but of accessing what has always been. It is a way of deprogramming your social conditioning to claim your natural inheritance of direct knowing.

The truth is, you always know the truth in your heart. You can hide it from yourself and you can deny it, but you can never completely separate yourself from the natural state of knowing it, feeling it, and being it.

To help strengthen that innate connection, we can turn to a well-known technique for accessing heart wisdom: the practice of meditation.

## WHAT IS MEDITATION?

Meditation is quite simply the practice of just being. It is easy to comprehend, but challenging to implement.

We live in an increasingly noisy world in our equally noisy minds. We have identified with our occupations and busyness for so long it has become an ingrained habit. Naturally, there will be some resistance to changing that and shifting into stillness.

At first, it can be awkward to embody the peaceful, quiet state of just being. It seems counter-intuitive, perhaps, but when we haven't practiced, it can be very difficult to sit still and relax without doing anything. That's okay. In fact, it's the perfect opportunity to observe your mind, where it tends to go, and what thoughts it tends to think.

It's also the perfect opportunity to practice compassion for yourself and release judgments about what you think your meditation experience should be. Even if you witness an internal dialogue like this:

"Stop thinking. Stop thinking."

"Ugh, why can't I stop thinking?"

"I must be insane. What is wrong with me?"

"Okay, focus on the breath, focus on the breath."

"Inhale, two, three, four...exhale, two, three, four."

"What the hell. I suck at this."

"Shhhh, it's okay. Just focus."

"I should get that meditation app."

"Ugh, shut up!"

"My back hurts."


Guess what? You are not alone. You are not a failure. You have succeeded in witnessing your mind jumping from thought to thought. That is an excellent observation. You may have also noticed a tendency to judge yourself. Again, very good information to have, because how can you make a conscious choice if you aren't even aware of what the options are?


## BENEFITS OF MEDITATION

Besides the benefits of getting to know our minds better, practicing compassion, and releasing attachments, some of the many side benefits of meditation include increased ability to concentrate, decreased stress, increased physical, emotional, and mental healing, increased feeling of well-being and peace, increased resilience in times of crisis, increased quality of sleep and rest, and increased freedom from painful psychological and behavioral patterns.

I'm not a scientist or a doctor, so I can only share what I've found to be true for me and the folks I've worked with, so as with everything I present in this book, I encourage you to experiment and see for yourself what the benefits are for you.

The reason why meditation is so healing is because in meditation practice, we are holding a loving space for ourselves and whatever is arising in the present moment. This space of acceptance is healing, because it is a demonstration of being open to what is. That's what love does. That's what consciousness does.

When we *be* the space of loving acceptance, we automatically dis-identify as the ego and the binds of our attachments, judgments, and stories begin to dissolve. As the psychic clutter clears, we experience more mental clarity and even more spaciousness. In this expanded clarity and spaciousness, we are able to discern our intuitive guidance. In the stillness of space, we can hear the whispers of spirit.

So, you see, it is a practice of receiving and allowing. Receiving all aspects of your self, allowing spaciousness, receiving guidance, allowing stillness, receiving the gift of the present moment, receiving love. Through a meditation practice, not only do we receive benefits for our physical, emotional, and mental bodies, we also open up to receive the gifts of spirit that will assist us in lightwork and life.

Eventually, your life will be like a meditation, infused with mindfulness, compassion, and peace. And after all, isn't that the goal of any technique? The point isn't to get really good at meditation or whatever the technique is, but to bring what you learn from the technique —that practice of present moment awareness and unconditional love—into every moment of your life. The tools are just a way to get you there.

## MEDITATION PREPARATION

There are as many forms of meditation as you can imagine. Below you will find some simple yet powerful ones to start. Remember, with technique it is all about the experience, so allow some time to really feel into the practice.

Reading and understanding intellectually is less than one percent of the practice; in other words, completely insufficient.

Since meditation is the practice of simply being, nothing is required. However, there are a few props you may enjoy experimenting with. You can try meditating in silence, and you can try listening to relaxing music or sound-healing tones. You may find it helpful to have a timer to facilitate turning off that part of your mind that wonders or worries about how long it's been. You could try a free meditation app. Some have interval timers that can be nice for reminding you to return to your breath or whatever your focus is.

It's helpful to carve out some private time and space so that you won't be interrupted, but even an interruption can be part of the medicine of acceptance of what's happening in the present moment. Remember, resisting what is happening in the moment will simply extend the time spent in suffering.

Many times in the past I have caught myself getting upset by the neighbor's noisy leaf blower or the dog barking when I was in session, but now I laugh. I give thanks for these things, because I appreciate the opportunity to let go, to choose a more loving thought, and to be more accepting. When I can laugh, I affirm that a particular situation has no power to take away my peace.

You can sit or lay on a cushion, a mat, a piece of furniture, the floor, or the earth. It doesn't really matter, and eventually you can practice anywhere. Some folks like to sit in an area that is only used for meditation because it signals, "it's meditation time," which you might find helpful if you have the space to do that. I personally like to mix it up and practice in different situations, because I recognize that reliance on props, spaces, or what other people are doing with their leaf blowers can eventually become disempowering. For me it is helpful to have a balance of some structured sanctuary and some chaotic conditions so I can work on mental flexibility. See what works for you and be aware that it could change from day to day.

You may appreciate being swaddled in a cozy blanket or having one nearby as you will most likely cool down somewhat while you are sitting or lying in stillness, especially if it is a longer meditation. A journal may also come in handy for information or inspiration that comes through in your meditation sessions.

If you are new to the practice of meditation, start with short periods of time—like five minutes—then gradually increase as you become more able to just be. Don't underestimate the power of being present and still for even a short period of time. In just one moment of presence, you enter the eternal.

For the following meditation technique experiments, read through the instructions for each exercise first, then give it a go. Don't worry about the specific steps or if if you're doing it right. Allow yourself to soak in the frequency of the intention.

## EXERCISE :: MEDITATION ON THE BREATH

**1.** Find a comfortable seated position and shift your weight to find a place of balance with the spine straight and shoulders relaxed. (You can lie down if sitting is uncomfortable.)
**2.** Begin to shift your focus from thinking to feeling.
**3.** Feel your breath moving in and out.
**4.** Notice the sensations in your body.
**5.** Notice the quality of the inhalation.
**6.** Notice the quality of the exhalation.
**7.** As you breathe, allow the breath to slow and deepen.
**8.** If your mind wanders into thinking, refocus its attention to observing the sensations of the body and noticing the qualities of the breath.
**9.** Keep coming back to feeling and breathing.
**10.** When your practice is complete, stretch, drink some water, and journal if you like.

## EXERCISE :: MEDITATION ON THE LIGHT

**1.** Find a comfortable seated position and shift your weight to find a place of balance with the spine straight and shoulders relaxed. (You can lie down if sitting is uncomfortable.)

**2.** Feel your breath moving in and out.

**3.** Notice what it feels like in your body.

**4.** As you breathe and relax, imagine a point of light on the top of your head.

**5.** Focus your attention on the light as you breathe.

**6.** Notice the quality of the light, its vibration, its flavor.

**7.** Keep breathing and observing the light.

**8.** If your mind wanders to thinking, gently guide it back to observing the breath and the light.

**9.** When your practice is complete, stretch, drink some water, and journal if you like.

Note: you can alternately focus on a point of light at your heart center, or in the center of your head. See if the different locations have different impressions or feelings.

### EXERCISE :: MEDITATION ON BREATHING LIGHT

This exercise is a combination of focusing on the breath and the light simultaneously.

**1.** Find a comfortable seated position and shift your weight to find a place of balance with the spine straight and shoulders relaxed. (You can lie down if sitting is uncomfortable.)

**2.** Feel your breath moving in and out.

**3.** Notice what it feels like in your body.

**4.** As you breathe and relax, imagine a point of light on the crown of your head.

**5.** Focus your attention on the light as you breathe.

**6.** Now, as you inhale, imagine the light on the crown of your head moving down into your heart.

**7.** As you exhale, imagine the light in your heart moving up to your crown.

**8.** Inhale and move the light from the crown to the heart.

**9.** Exhale and move the light from the heart to the crown.

**10.** Keep breathing and moving the light down and up with the breath.

**11.** If your mind wanders to thinking, gently guide it back to observing the breath and the light.

**12.** When your practice is complete, stretch, drink some water, and journal if you like.


## EXERCISE :: MEDITATION ON LOVING KINDNESS

**1.** Find a comfortable position and shift your weight to find a place of balance with the spine straight and shoulders relaxed. (You can lie down if sitting is uncomfortable.)

**2.** Feel your breath moving in and out.

**3.** Notice what it feels like in your body.

**4.** Soften the face, the jaw, the eyes, maybe even have the feeling of a gentle smile on the inside.

**5.** As you breathe, feel into the love in your heart, perhaps recalling times you felt kind and loving.

**6.** Breathe and feel the love within you, feel your capacity for love.

**7.** Feel the energy of your heart growing stronger as you focus on the feeling of love.

**8.** Allow yourself to feel this love for yourself.

**9.** Keep breathing and feeling this loving kindness.

**10.** On the inhale, say to yourself silently, "I am loved."

**11.** On the exhale say to yourself silently, "I am love."

**12.** Keep breathing and feeling.

**13.** If your mind wanders to thinking, gently guide it back to observing the breath, the feeling, and the words, "I am loved," and, "I am love".

**14.** When your practice is complete, stretch, drink some water, and journal if you like.

Practice at least one of the previous meditations before moving on to the next section.

## JOURNEY MEDITATION

This technique requires a bit more explanation before beginning and is best to do after trying some of the shorter meditations first.

A journey meditation is simply going somewhere intentionally in your imagination with a specific focus or goal in mind. The ideal mindstate is trance-like and feels like being in a lucid dream without being asleep.

When meditating, the brain slows its roll from the beta brainwave state of talking and thinking to the alpha state of relaxation. Alpha is the light meditation state. The deeper meditation state occurs when the brain slows down even more into theta waves. Theta is the mode of lucid dreaming and is ideal for journeying. You will most likely vacillate between alpha and beta when you first start meditating, but as you practice you'll be able to drop into alpha quickly and from there move into theta.

For the following exercise, you will practice a journey meditation to become comfortable with the process. To keep track of time, you can use a music or drum track about 8 minutes in length or a timer set for 8 minutes. Once you practice it for 8 minutes, you can extend to longer periods of time.

There are the several intentions for the following journey exercise:

• To travel to a place of healing, wisdom, and peace within you, so that you may have a direct experience of already embodying and therefore having access to wisdom, wholeness, and peace.
• To teach, through experience, the steps of an effective journey.
• To provide an opportunity for you to practice receiving information from your inner teacher.
• To experience a powerful technique for grounding your energy and healing your body.
• To practice using one of your most powerful tools: your imagination.

## LISTENING TO THE INNER TEACHER

The inner teacher, what I sometimes refer to as the voice of spirit or the unified self, speaks softly. So softly, in fact, that you may not be accustomed to hearing its whispers over the louder voice of the separate-self or ego. You can only hear one voice at a time. If you're hearing a disempowering fear-based thought, you are listening to the voice of the ego. If you're hearing an empowering love-based thought, you are listening to the voice of your higher self, the self that knows it is one with unified consciousness.

It's really very simple. Do your thoughts result in feelings of peace and purpose or upset and fear? The inner teacher, your true nature, will always be loving. Even when its messages are urgent, they will feel calm, grounded and purposeful. And when you think those thoughts, you will experience peace.

If you hear fear-based thoughts, don't worry. Those thoughts have no power over you. If you see fearful images, don't worry, those images have no power over you. It's all just information and most likely not yours and/or something coming up to clear/heal. To get clarity, you can ask the questions in the **Mental Discernment** section earlier in this chapter.

One of the intentions for the journey exercise is to practice receiving guidance from our inner teacher. As you will see, sometimes the inner teacher speaks in words, sometimes in pictures, sometimes in a knowingness. Through our practice we will learn to trust the messages we receive.

## PREPARING FOR JOURNEY MEDITATION

To prepare for this meditation, allow yourself some time without interruption, to tune in, to listen, and to record your thoughts afterward. You will benefit from having a comfortable place to lie down and totally relax. It is also helpful to have your notebook close at hand to record any interesting things you may experience.

Because the voice of spirit often speaks in a symbolic language similar to the imagery of dreams, sometimes it will make sense to your logical mind and sometimes it won't. It can be helpful during meditation to cultivate an open mindstate and receive any messages, images, awareness, or knowingness without the need for it to make sense or appear in a certain form.

Like recording dreams, it is best to simply record what you experienced exactly as you recall it and then, if you like, you can go back and read it for possible insights later. It may be that you have an understanding of the symbolism immediately, or it may only become clear at a much later point in time. Perhaps it will remain a mystery forever. That's okay, too.

However it may seem to be to your intellectual understanding, you can be sure that subconsciously the message has been delivered and received. You can also be assured that attachment to figuring it out, or the specialness of it, or the significance of it is not helpful in the least. What is helpful is embracing the mystery and the magic of your imagination.

Any time you journey, it is helpful to plan out your path ahead of time. In the following meditation exercise we will use the basic plan of fundamental journey steps:

**1.** Start in a power place.
**2.** Enter a pre-determined path.
**3.** Go to a safe space.
**4.** Receive the medicine.
**5.** Come back the way you came.
**6.** End where you began.

Before beginning your journey practice, read through the directions, then drop into the meditation. The steps for the process follow below.

## EXERCISE :: GO ON A JOURNEY

**1.** Start with setting a clear intention that you are journeying for the purposes of connecting with and receiving healing energy from your higher self/inner teacher.
**2.** Set a timer (or music track) for 8 minutes (or longer as you build your practice.)
**3.** Lie down, close your eyes, relax, and breathe.

**4.** Begin in a power place: Imagine yourself on high ground in a beautiful forest. In this power place you feel happy, grounded, and safe. Decide on this place before you begin and get a good idea of it in your mind.

**5.** Imagine a pathway: For now, use a footpath that leads from the starting place down into the forest. The path goes down, down, down, deeper and deeper into the forest and leads to a protected space.

**6.** Go to a protected space: For this meditation, make it a magical circle of ancient trees. When you get to the circle of trees, sit or lie down and imagine you are in a place of safety and power, a place outside of ordinary consciousness, a place where you can connect with your higher self and source consciousness.

**7.** Receive the medicine: In the magical circle, you can relax and open to receive healing energy, messages, symbols or feelings from your higher self. Allow yourself to receive impressions without analyzing them.

**8.** Come back the way you came: When you hear the timer go off or the music end, give thanks to the trees and all the beings of light, travel back up, up, up the path, coming back to your starting place.

**9.** Finish in the place you started: Take a breath in your power place to draw all your energy back, feel grateful, then open your eyes when you're ready.

**10.** Journal: Immediately write in your journal any impressions you had. Sometimes by writing you will remember things you wouldn't have thought of otherwise.

**11.** Take a moment to transition, drink water, and stretch your body.

Because there are many ways you can apply the journey meditation tool in lightwork, learning it will support the growth of your practice. Since ancient times, seekers around the world have embarked on both mental and physical journeys for information gathering, spiritual initiations, giving and receiving healings, and more. Each and every one of us has the information of ancestral ways encoded in our DNA. To practice journeying is to awaken this ancestral knowledge.

When you first start, it is important to have a structure so you don't get lost on the astral plane somewhere, but once you master the technique you can freestyle. For now, stick with the simple steps: get clear on your intention, know the power place where you're going to start and end, and stay on the same path going in and coming back.

Once you're clear on your intentions, relax and enjoy practicing the journey meditation. Trust that nothing you can do is wrong and whatever happens is perfect.

## CHAPTER 4 :: KEY POINTS

- Intuition is natural.
- Denial will block intuition.
- Denial can be released through willingness.
- The more you practice following intuition the more you will trust it.
- Dropping your mind into your heart will help you to feel and know the truth.
- You will recognize the truth because it is already within you.
- Meditational practices will help you access inner wisdom.
- Meditation helps you access present moment awareness.
- The key to mastery is to practice presence in daily life.
- Journey meditation is a way to access inner teachings.

## CHAPTER 4 :: INTEGRATION TIPS

- Practice dropping into your heart space at different times in the day: while eating a meal, listening to someone speak, riding the bus, or brushing your teeth.
- During a walk, feel into your surroundings. Really pay attention to details while also allowing your awareness to expand out hundreds of feet in all directions.
- When you're at work, feel into the earth below you, the sky above you, or the trees. Feel into your connection with nature wherever you are.

## CHAPTER 4 :: PRACTICUM POSSIBILITIES

**Intuitive inventory:** (5 - 10 minutes)

What are some examples of intuitive language that you've experienced? How does it speak to you? Is it through pictures? Feelings? Make a list of all the ways you've experienced intuitive information being relayed.

What are some times in your life when you felt connected or disconnected to your intuition? Were there times you followed it? Were there times you didn't follow it? What happened?

Take a moment to reflect on the questions. By pausing and journaling you may find you remember more specific details.

**Explore tools from the meditation:** (about 5 minutes each)

Throughout this week, take some time to practice the tools from the meditation. For a few minutes, relax, close your eyes, and imagine you are doing the following:

- Connecting with the earth in a power place.
- Resting in the sacred grove of the forest.
- Growing energetic roots and branches like a tree.
- Conversing with a mineral, plant, or animal spirit that you may have met in the meditation.
- Communing with your higher self.

**Expand to new media:** (as long as you like)

Artfully expand on an aspect or aspects of your meditational journey experience through a different medium. Some suggestions to get you started:

- Draw or paint pictures of images you saw in the meditation.
- Make up a tune or song that sounds like part of the meditation.
- Write a short scene based on characters from the meditation.
- Create a dance that reminds you of a feeling in the meditation.

# PART TWO

## MULTIMODALITY ENERGY WORK TECHNIQUES

**You are the flame**


you are not
your body
your thoughts
or emotions

you are not
your past
your beliefs
or your trauma

you are
the eternal flame
of spirit

a holy child
wholly innocent

a force of nature
already perfect
already free

like the sun
your shining
is an act of creation

# CHAPTER 5:
# INVOCATION + CO-CREATION

*All knowledge exists in the one mind we share*

## LIGHTHEARTEDNESS

No matter your age or circumstance, you are a child of the universe. You have an infinite capacity for creating in unconditional love. You get to create whatever feels truly joyful for you. You get to imagine yourself returning to a state of original innocence before anyone told you that you were not enough. Consider this moment as one of your infinite chances to reclaim a sense of being perfect just as you are.

As we begin our exploration into the realms of energy work, let's remember that our essential nature is pure consciousness. In pure consciousness, there is no right or wrong or good or bad. Holding this truth in our mind, we are able to engage in whatever work we do with a lightness that allows us to shift vast amounts of energy with ease.

If instead we choose to operate from a mindset that there is something that is wrong and must be fixed, or something that is right and must be attained, we will be engaging in unnecessary resistance or craving that is common in the mentality of lack. Resistance of what is or craving what isn't are huge energy drains. You might like to use that energy for something else.

Healing and learning can certainly be intense, but as we open to feel and heal more pain, we are also opening our hearts to feel more joy. Feelings of joy, peace, and gratitude strengthen our hearts and create resilience for the long haul. To get to a place of joyful creativity, we can focus our energy more on what we'd like to create in the world, rather than what we wouldn't like. We can choose to return to a state of child-like curiosity, creativity, and playfulness. We can choose to heal our hearts, let them release their heaviness and open to feel more love again.

**Staying in your open heart is a revolutionary act.**

It is healing. It is powerful. It is the key to resilience that will support a vibrant, purposeful life of living your spiritual practice in the world.

It is important that we acknowledge the social conditioning that taught us to shut down our hearts and be fearful, because the most common blocks I see arising in people's minds when they step into this work are those related to fear, especially fear of making mistakes that cause more pain. In society's institutional and family systems we were taught that if we make a mistake or don't know the answer, we are wrong/guilty, and we deserve to fail/be punished.

I reject these programs of fear and I invite you to affirm the following with me:

• Nothing you can do is wrong.
• Everything is for your learning and growth.
• You can learn through play.
• Lightwork is play.
• This is all an experiment.
• There is no failure. Ever.

Take a breath and receive that. Receive it for your inner child.

Now let's play.

## MULTIMODALITY ENERGY WORK

Multimodality energy work is how I describe my toolkit of techniques from multiple modalities, or styles, of energy work. I think of it as a painter's palette with different colors with which to paint. Each lightwork session is a unique co-creation. Different circumstances call for different tools.

For example, sometimes I choose mental techniques, sometimes I choose manual ones, and sometimes I choose to guide the client through a visualization in which they perform the action themselves. The tool I choose depends on the context and what my intuition is showing me in the moment.

There are times when it is more helpful to work quickly, others when it is more helpful to slow down. There are times when it is more helpful to teach a client a technique through words, and times when it is more helpful to let them receive the teaching on an experiential level. With practice, you will become more skillful at knowing the most beneficial approach for any given situation.

The reason I teach a combination of multiple energy work modalities is because I've yet to find one that covers all situations and achieves the desired effects with maximum efficiency. That doesn't mean that choosing to work only one modality is wrong, it's just not my way. You are free to take these teachings and apply them in a way that feels potent for you.

Along with a combination of various energy work tools, I teach a combination of structured protocol and intuitive flow. I've found that combination most supportive for my work, and for the work of my students. The Lightwork Session Protocol outline in the **Appendix** gives a strong foundation of best practices on which to structure your work, and the tools in **Chapter 4: Development of Intuition** help you build trust in your intuitive guidance so that you can go with the flow of a session and follow the energy wherever it is leading.

If you ground yourself in solid structure and form and maintain mental agility and flexibility, you will embody a powerful technique. If you are too rigid and dogmatic, or too fluid and formless, you will lack the opposing energies that create balance and centering. If we stay centered, there is an ability to move in any direction. Neutrality opens the way to more possibility and choice.


## LOVE IS THE HEALER

The only preparation that is absolutely essential for doing energy work is a willingness to release anything that doesn't allow you to do it, which means releasing the blocks to love. Love is the healer. Separate from love, we cannot heal. Separation is the thought-system of the ego. Ego cannot heal, just as separation cannot make whole.

As we discovered in **Chapter 3: Mindset Awareness**, you have a separate-self or egoic belief system that is confused, alone, and afraid. You also have a true-self or unified mind state that is clear, connected, and powerful. The separation never really occurred, but if you *believe* it did, you will make up an illusory reality that upholds that belief system.

When we identify as the ego, we struggle with feelings of lack and limitation. Those are the hallmarks of a separation mindset. To do this work successfully, we must be willing to let go of those limiting beliefs and allow infinite love to flow through us.

Fortunately, we needn't worry ourselves about how to do this, because our unified mind already knows. And the part of our mind that worries, doubts, and tries to figure things out in vain can never know. It *must* not ever know, because that would spell its end.

Therefore, we will practice setting aside that always-thinking-never-knowing part of our mind and choose instead the sane, all-knowing mind of love. As always, our willingness is all that is required to make the shift, but with the technique of invocation described in this chapter, we will develop a more formalized practice for shifting from separation-thinking to unity consciousness.

## A NOTE ON WORDS

As I mention at various points in this text, it is important not to get too hung up on the specific forms of words, but rather to follow the energy underlying the words. Words are symbols of thoughts, which are symbolic of things. Therefore, they are symbols twice removed from the thing itself. They are not the thing itself. That being said, I'd like to clarify a bit about my word usage.

I will sometimes use the following words interchangeably to signify a similar energy: nature, truth, universal law, true self, consciousness, spirit, the one mind, love.

And I will sometimes use these words interchangeably to signify a different energy: belief, lies, the world, illusion, separation, insanity, false self, ego.

You can no doubt feel the difference in the energy of these two lists. So, if at some point I say "spirit" and at another I say "love" and in yet another I say "true nature" or "unified mind" you will know I am speaking to the underlying energy these things have in common. Same with the second list. There's a Zen koan I read a long time ago that said, "If you can say what it is, that's not it." I think of that whenever I'm trying to describe something in words that can't be grasped intellectually, only experientially.

For most of my life, I refused to use the word "god" to describe the energy of universal life force energy/consciousness, because it was too loaded with negative emotional baggage for me. When I was new on the lightwork path, in the Pranic Healing clinic, we would do a meditation that started with an invocation "to the supreme god." Every time I heard it I would feel a little contraction inside. You could say I had god issues.

It wasn't just the word "god" either. In my early twenties, there were a few years in which I refused to use the word "love" or tell anyone "I love you." The way I saw it, what people called "love" was actually a lot more like obligation, possessiveness, co-dependency, or lust. So, I protested by boycotting a word about whose meaning people obviously had no clue. And I was definitely one of those clueless people.

It took a lot of willingness to reopen my heart. It took years of inquiry, self-help books, holistic healing, and practice before I felt that I might have a chance at being truly loving and loved. Slowly, "love" came back into my usage, but it took that spiritual initiation of almost dying in the hospital to bring me back around to being willing - cringingly at first - to use the word "god" again.

So, you know, I get it. I get how words can be charged with all kinds of multi-layered personal meaning and emotional triggers. I get how some of the words I use might sound like a bunch of new age mumbo jumbo. And some might feel like they are breaking your heart open. Notice what has potency for you.

In short, use words that feel good to you. Sometimes feeling good means keeping it light, sometimes it means breaking out the heavy hitters. Trust in the way the energy feels to you in the moment, because it's your practice and only you know what feels true for you.

As with all things in the world of form, the words and other symbols you choose to signal your intentions will no doubt change over time. What's important is the energy behind the form.

## INVOCATION

Invocation initiates a process, like toppling the first in a series of dominoes. The tool itself is simple to practice, yet so profound that if you use it consistently it will change your life forever.

Invocation is not only the first step in the Lightwork Session Protocol, but it's also the simplest, most powerful, and most versatile tool in the Lightworker Training toolkit. You can use it for anything you can imagine. I teach it at the beginning of the section on energy work so that you will have a workable tool for any energetic phenomenon you may encounter in a session.

Invocational techniques are my go-to practice throughout the day and throughout a healing session. Invocation is a complete healing in and of itself. It is healing because it works through our willingness to tap into the infinite power and presence of love as the healer.

When we use invocation to access the mindstate of unity consciousness, we can be assured that the work we perform will be coming from a place of love, our intentions will have powerful effects, the effects will be for the highest and best of all that is, and they will come into manifestation with grace and ease.

So what exactly is invocation, and how do we use it?

To invoke is to call in or summon. It is an intentional or mental practice performed silently or vocally. There are many schools of thought on what the most potent type of invocation is. Some practitioners call upon deities, angels, or elemental beings. Some invoke their teachers, ancestors, and gurus. I like to go straight to the source of all that is, because in my experience it is the most clear, direct, powerful, and effective technique.

Incidentally, I've found that even if you choose to work with angels, deities, and spiritual helpers, it is energetically cleaner if you invoke source energy first. Source doesn't require energy exchange, because it is all energy everywhere, so you won't accrue energetic debt or entanglement the way you can if you go through the spiritual hierarchy. That being said, if you ask source to send a helper, you can choose to offer gratitude to that helper. A heartfelt "thank you" is a gift that all teachers, ancestors, guides, and helpers appreciate.

The organic light of source energy is the consciousness that is flowing through all things in the multiverse. Because we are extensions of that light/consciousness, all that is required to tap into it is to remember that we are it. In this space of remembrance, we are empowered and our intentions are effective.

Because we spend so much time identified with limiting beliefs such as thinking we are our bodies, separate from spirit, prone to harm, and lacking in power, it can be helpful to use a tool like invocation to make the deliberate shift from our separate-self mindstate to the infinite mind of unity consciousness where all minds are joined. With invocation we *re-mind* ourselves.

Let's look at some specifics of how we can consciously shift energy through the power of our mind and invocation.

## 3-PART PRAYER POWER

Invocation is a kind of prayer. It may be very different from other prayers you've encountered. It does not ask for something that is wanting. There's no supplication or entreaty. Prayers of entreaty often unconsciously affirm lack. Affirming lack is not helpful if you'd like to feel the abundant manifestation of whatever you are praying for.

There are three essential parts to a truly effective invocation or prayer:

**1.** Shift to the unified mind.
**2.** State a clear intention.
**3.** Give thanks.

Let's break them down one-by-one.

## SHIFT TO THE UNIFIED MIND

There are many ways of shifting from a mindset of separation to identifying as one with the infinite mind where all minds are joined. Some may feel more effective than others. Your preferences may change as you go and that's totally cool. The most important thing is to follow the energy of what feels potent for you at any given time and circumstance.

Here are some of the ways I like to shift to the unified mind:

• Place my hand on my heart and remember that I am the embodiment of infinite love.

- Remember that I am not alone, that I am one with all that is.
- Call upon my higher/holy spirit self to take charge.
- Imagine my crown/heart connected to source consciousness with a golden channel of light.
- Remember I am a force of nature, connected to everything in the web of life.

Give some of these a try. You can speak out loud, silently, or use a gesture. Maybe you say, "I am one with the one/my higher self" Maybe you take a deep breath and feel your connection to the Earth. Practice feeling into which ways are strong for you. You can use whatever names, feelings, or visuals for source consciousness you prefer. What feels powerful to you in this moment?

## STATE A CLEAR INTENTION

Once you have shifted to the unified mind you are in a state of co-creation with the universe, so you simply state a clear intention of what you are choosing to create. Remember, if you are one with the oneness of all life, you lack for nothing. If you lack for nothing, you don't need to ask for anything.

Therefore, it is more helpful to set intentions to release whatever is blocking you from knowing, being, or receiving what you'd like to experience rather than ask for what you want. The oneness wants for nothing because it is everything.

Here are some of my favorite intentions:

- "I am releasing this unloving thought now."
- "I am willing to release all my judgments about this now."
- "I am willing to be willing to let this go."
- "I am willing to release anything that doesn't allow this healing."
- "I am clearing my many bodies of anything that no longer serves me."
- "I am healing this through all dimensions of time and space."
- "I am grateful to share my healing with everyone."

- "I am clearing anything that doesn't allow my liberation."

Can you feel how clear and powerful those are? What are some other powerful intentions you can create?

## GIVE THANKS

This is essential because gratitude is what we feel when we know something is done. When we know our burden has been lifted, we feel grateful. We feel joyful and thankful. We feel the energy of "Yes!" Having a feeling of gratitude in your body brings the energy of what you're creating into the physical world.

Here are some simple ways to express—or be—the energy of thanks:

- Say or think a heart-felt "thank you."
- Say or think "It is done/so it is/amen."
- Say or think "I am so glad."
- Smile.
- Breathe a sigh of relief.
- Feel the light of your heart/your spirit/the sun/source.
- Laugh in joy.
- Cry in gratitude.

These are all simple, yet powerful. Whatever way feels authentic in the moment, go for it. As long as the energy of gratitude and completion is woven into your prayers, they will be effective, because gratitude is what we feel when something is accomplished.

The three simple steps of mind shift, intention, and gratitude are all it takes to create a powerful invocation that will clear any kind of energetic block you can imagine. Invocations don't have to be long and complicated to be effective.

A wonderful thing about this prayer practice is that we can heal whatever is causing our suffering all the way back to the root cause, without ever having to re-experience it or relive the trauma. That's what I call grace.

## THE POWER OF GRATITUDE

Gratitude is not only essential for effective intentional work, like prayer and invocation, it is also a powerful practice to weave into your daily practice to create the life you desire. Gratitude is what closes the gap that appears to be between what you are experiencing now and what you'd like to experience.

If you'd like to create a situation in which something is done, you must focus on feeling of it already being done. In the present moment, imagine what it feels like when the process is already completed and you are enjoying the end result. Remember, the present moment is where all creation happens, so if we'd like to heal something, we must focus our minds on imagining what it would feel like to be already healed right now.

This is where many folks get tripped up, because they are focusing on the problem of what they don't want to experience, rather than the feeling of what they *would* like. Focusing on lack in the present will only create more lack in the future. Yes, you can acknowledge what is happening in the present, but dwelling on painful thoughts will only sap your energy and make it harder to create the situation that you'd like.

It may seem counter-intuitive in the moment to give thanks for healing when you feel unwell and miserable, but this is how universal law works. Consciousness is the light that illuminates and gives life to whatever is in its path. You can use your mind to focus and imagine what you'd like to experience and consciousness will give it life. If you'd like to experience healing, focus on that instead of the symptoms of the illness.

When we are focusing on the energy of the result we'd like to experience, we will feel it and create more of it. The feeling is what is important. The energy of being grateful is more important than the words you use, if any, so I encourage you to play around with ways to tap into that feeling. Perhaps you remember a time when you felt overwhelmingly grateful or a time you felt like you were completely in the flow of abundance. You can use that memory to jumpstart your gratitude feeling.

Here are some of the ways to practice gratitude:

• Feel grateful that you don't have to figure out how to make the universe/ your body/the Earth function.
• Think about all of nature supporting you freely and unconditionally.
• Think about all of your ancestors/spirit guides/angels supporting you freely and unconditionally.
• Think about how all the true and beautiful things in life are free and unconditional.

## SPIRITUAL BYPASSING

Since we've been talking about focusing our imaginations on what we would like to experience rather than focusing on the perceived problem, it feels important here to talk a bit about spiritual bypassing.

Let's be clear that harnessing and focusing the power of our minds is different than trying to avoid dealing with something. When we attempt to skip steps, gloss over, avoid feeling uncomfortable, or resist doing the actual work of our practices, that's called spiritual bypassing.

Spiritual bypassing is a form of resisting what is. It's a form of avoiding doing the spiritual work. If we avoid doing our spiritual, mental, emotional, and physical work, it will be obvious in the energy of how it feels. Spiritual bypassing always feels false and disempowering. Like a fake smile, spiritual bypassing takes the surface form of something that it isn't. It might look at first glance like enlightenment, but under the surface appearance the energy is not one of love and compassion. It is one of fear. Love wouldn't try to avoid, resist, or gloss over something painful, but fear sure would.

Every day we experience or witness things that are painful. Every day we have an opportunity to shift our perspective of that pain. Not to deny it, bury it, hide it, or avoid it, but to be present with it, breathe into it, acknowledge it, and bless it with our love and compassion. This is healing.

Avoidance is not healing, nor is being overly identified with pain and trauma. Clinging to an old wound is another extreme on the clinging/avoiding spectrum. The spectrum is thought of as linear, but circular would be more accurate, as the extremes have more in common with each other than one might think. For example, clinging can actually be a means of avoiding moving forward and avoidance can be a means of clinging to where one is at.

The uncertainty inherent in change can trigger a fear-based response of avoiding or clinging, but, thankfully, evolution is happening whether we like it or not.

## CONSCIOUSNESS IS EVOLVING

Consciousness is ever-evolving. Avoiding and clinging are painful because they attempt to block the evolution of consciousness. To understand more about how we get stuck, it can be helpful to look at the phases in the cycle of evolving consciousness. Here's how those phases relate to healing:

**1.** Awareness: identifying the thing you'd like to heal.
**2.** Healing: doing the work to heal it.
**3.** Teaching: sharing the healing, which brings more awareness, which starts the cycle again.

The shadow side of phase one is overly identifying with the-unhealed-one, the wounded aspect of the self. The shadow side of phase two is overly identifying with the-healing-one, getting stuck in a pattern of always working the same lesson over and over. The shadow side of phase three is overly identifying as the-one-who-has-healed and not recognizing there is more work to do.

If we get stuck in any one of the phases, we are attempting to block the evolution of consciousness. We might be afraid of taking that next step. Perhaps we believe that staying where we are is more comfortable than changing. Oftentimes, we get stuck because we think we have to figure out how to do something before we can do it.

As mentioned before, thinking you have to figure out how to do something before you do it is a trap, because knowing how to do it comes *after* doing it. First you choose something, then you do it, *then* you know how.

With invocation, you can release your worry about not knowing how and tap into the infinite mind where all things are known. You can trust that whatever your intention is will be done in the perfect way. As you practice, the order in which ideas become manifested into form will become abundantly clear.

So, without further ado, let's get into it with some practical examples that illustrate how you can use invocation.

## EXAMPLES OF INVOCATIONS

As mentioned earlier, invocation is a type of intentional practice that taps into the power of the infinite mind we share. 3-part prayer power is a simple template you can use to create effective invocations. You can put the energy of all three parts into one sentence, which is the kind of simple invocation I like to do throughout the day.

Here are some examples:

- "I am so grateful to receive and follow my guidance today. Thank you."
- "I am grateful to surrender to the holy altar fire whatever this suffering is and allow it to be transmuted all the way back to the root cause, and so it is."
- "I am grateful to choose peace now, and anything that doesn't allow peace I'm releasing through all dimensions of time and space. So be it."
- "I am surrendering this situation to the one mind in perfect trust. So grateful to let it be and so it is."
- "I am so thankful that I am one with the infinite mind where all things are known."
- "Thank you, spirit, for helping me to see myself/this person/this circumstance/everything through eyes of love."

## A NOTE ON PRAYING FOR OTHERS

Did you notice the last invocation in the list above? Check it out. This type of wording and thinking is infinitely more helpful than an intention that affirms lack. When praying for others, the most effective prayer is one in which we affirm the inherent perfection in them. To be truly helpful, we must release our judgment that something is wrong.

If we judge someone as wrong and needing to be fixed, we are using the power of our minds to energize exactly what we don't want. Rather than seek to change the person we judge as broken, we seek to change our minds about them. The most powerful way I know to hold space for healing of another is to heal my mind about them, hold that vision no matter what, and allow that person to come into resonance with me, if they choose.

When we shift our thinking, miraculous change can happen. Our minds are powerful, because they are animated with source consciousness, so if we use them to affirm another's lack or energize the perceived problem, we will attract and experience more of that ourselves. But, when we take responsibility for releasing our opinions, judgments, and fear-based thoughts that aren't helping anyone, we free ourselves of those limiting beliefs and we automatically share the benefits with everyone, because we share one mind.

Here's an example of a powerful way to pray for another person or yourself when you think something is wrong:

*"I am grateful to release all of my opinions and judgments about (person/situation), so that I may see it all through eyes of love.*

*I am grateful to know now the perfection of (person/situation) and share the benefits of my learning with everyone because we are one.*

*As I let it be, so it is. "*

In short, if you think you need to pray for someone or something else, pray for yourself first.

## INVOCATION APPLICATIONS

In sessions with my clients, I often use free-flowing, intuitive invocations which I say aloud so the client can be more conscious of the process and add their energy to the intention. I have found that vocalized invocations and going with the flow of the session feels right for me now that I have practiced a lot and trust my intuition. This wasn't always the case, however, and I started out doing formal, repetitive invocations silently in my mind, which also worked perfectly.

I didn't outgrow repetitive invocations so much as I became an embodied carrier of that frequency. That happens with all these tools. You use them so much, they become a part of you. It's getting to the point now where as soon as I become aware that something is coming up for healing, it immediately starts to release, because that's what I've been doing multiple times a day every day for over a decade. I've even had people report that they set an intention to work with me and energy starts shifting, or they see me in a dream and have a healing. This is the healing power of our minds and our intentions.

As a beginner, it is important to practice effective form, so that you will be imprinting yourself with the exact energy you'd like to eventually embody. To that effect, you will benefit from being precise and focused when first practicing invocations. As you begin to get comfortable with trusting your ability to partner up with universal intelligence and state clear intentions, your invocation process will become more of a quick, natural reflex.

You can use invocation for any of the steps of the Lightwork Session Protocol that we use as a guiding outline for session work. Below you will find the intentions for each step of session work. To use them, include the two other ingredients of shifting to unity consciousness and gratitude.

In the following invocation template, notice the three parts of a powerful prayer practice: shifting to the unified mind, stating a clear intention, and giving thanks.

## LIGHTWORKER INVOCATION TEMPLATE

*"Taking a breath of love and gratitude, I am thankful to be joined in my heart and mind with the one heart, the one mind of creation.*

*It is my intent that <u>(insert intention here)</u>.*

*I let it be and so it is."*

Here are some examples of intentions you can use to fill in the blank:

- **For setting the space at the beginning of a session**: "It is my intent that <u>(this person)</u> receive this healing in the perfect way in total grace and ease."
- **For clearing energy during a session**: "It is my intent that any and all energetic congestion be cleared from this (chakra/body/field) in the perfect way."
- **For clearing entities encountered during a session**: "It is my intent that any and all entities be cleared from <u>(this person)'s</u> many-bodied self through all dimensions of time/space and for anything that doesn't allow that to be cleared in the perfect way now."
- **For adding energy during a session**: "It is my intent that whatever frequencies are required  for <u>(energizing/balancing/stabilizing/harmonizing)</u> these energy fields be downloaded from the one mind now in gentleness and ease."
- **For closing a session**: "It is my intent that anything else that is required for the completion of this session be released or received now in the perfect way."

The possibilities for the tool of invocation are limited only by your imagination. It is not only useful when you don't know of any other way to do something, it is also immensely helpful when you do know, but are feeling stuck for some reason. In that moment, you can use invocation first to clear your personal attachments to whatever you're dealing with, and then use it again to perform the task that you are feeling unable to do.

We all have those times when we feel like we hit a wall and invocation is a tool that can shift the energy as if by magic. What follows is a story about how the tool of invocation supported me in my first session as a healer.

"We have a new healer today," my Pranic Healing teacher announced to the clinic as she put her arm around my shoulders.

"What?" I thought, my eyes widening in surprise. My expression must have shown I was neither feeling prepared nor qualified for the job. Her face lit up, "Don't worry, I'll be here if you need any help."

I had been coming to the donation-based Pranic Healing clinic for a couple months and assumed that on that day I would be receiving healing work as usual, but just three days prior, I had taken a beginner's Pranic Healing weekend intensive. Now my teacher was pushing me out of the nest.

At first, I was feeling a bit sorry for myself and the client assigned to me, but luckily, my client was another Pranic Healer who assured me, "You'll do great." I took a deep breath, closed my eyes, and invoked for divine assistance in the most heartfelt way I had ever invoked before.

Out of shyness and to help my focus, I kept my eyes closed while I worked and I surprised myself by not only remembering the order of all the steps in the healing protocol and how to do them, but also by feeling at ease as I worked.

To be sure, there were a few moments when I felt a sudden panic, "What if I'm wrong? What if I'm not reading this right? What if I fuck up?" And even though the fear and doubt would grip my stomach in that moment, somehow I would miraculously remember to stop, take a deep breath, and invoke again. And every time, without fail, my mind would settle enough to recognize that I could let go of that fear-based thought, I could trust in the beings of light helping me, and I could trust in the teachings I was following.

In the moments of invocation I somehow knew that even if I didn't feel like I could trust my own abilities, I could trust myself to get help from the highest source. And though at first it seemed horrifying to be put to work at clinic when I didn't think I knew what I was doing, I was grateful afterward for the opportunity to prove to myself that I could do it. My client confirmed it.

"I feel great," he said, "Really peaceful, more relaxed, and the pain is gone." I was astounded. My mind was all over the place, flip-flopping between celebration and cynicism, but behind all the chatter, there was a calm presence that seemed to say, "See, I told you it would be okay."

The power of invocation techniques to move stuck energies still amazes me, because even with over a decade of daily lightwork practice, every day I run into all kinds of energetic phenomena about which I know absolutely nothing. You will no doubt experience this yourself, if you haven't already. Therefore, I recommend experimenting with different applications to get comfortable using invocation in a variety of situations. That way, whatever comes up, you'll feel confident letting spirit do the heavy lifting for you.

Practice to see what feels powerful and authentic. Like any other part of your practice, the more you use invocation, the more you will experience its effects. With the experience of effects comes trust in effectiveness.

Practice can't make *you* any more perfect than you already are, but it can surely hone your lightwork skills to a level of mastery. Below you will find some colors from the lightwork palette you may choose to create with. Play around to see what feels most joyful and authentic for you. Remember, nothing you can do is wrong.

## CHAPTER 5 :: KEY POINTS

- You are a child of the universe.
- Invocation is a way to partner up with universal intelligence.
- Invocation initiates a process that eventually manifests in energetic and/or physical form.
- Invocation can be used alone or as the initiation of a larger process.
- Invocation can be stated aloud or silently.
- Invocation is a way of co-creating with the infinite mind where all minds are joined.

- Stating clear intentions makes invocations more powerful.
- Gratitude makes invocations more powerful.
- Invocation is a way of doing things you don't know how to do.
- No matter what arises in session, you can use invocation.


## CHAPTER 5 :: INTEGRATION TIPS

- In the morning, invoke to: ask for guidance and support throughout the day, or to set an intention of what you'd like to create.
- In the evening, invoke to: clear anyone else's energy from your body and fields, and reclaim your energy from any person, place, or situation.
- When you feel challenged, invoke to: shield your body's biofield from unwanted energies, and see the situation/yourself with eyes of love.


## CHAPTER 5 :: PRACTICUM POSSIBILITIES

**Daily Releasing Ritual:** (about 10 minutes)

At the end of the day, write down every upsetting feeling you can remember. Anything you felt that was anything less than unconditional love and acceptance. You may wish to also include unloving thoughts, although it can sometimes be easier to identify emotions.

Once you get your list, it's time to release all that stuff. Practice using this (or a similar) prayer:

*"Co-creating with the infinite mind of the universe, I am clearing all of these energies from my many-bodied self all the way back to the root cause. I am thankful and grateful to hand it over to the one mind and so it is."*

Try this experiment every day for a week or more and see what happens.


**Healing Protocol Practice:** (as long as you like)

It's time for your first session! No big deal, though, because you have the tool of invocation. For this exercise, you will demonstrate some of its many applications.

Your mission is to go through the Lightwork Session Protocol in the Appendix and practice performing each one of the steps in the outline with an invocation technique.

Use the Lightworker Invocation Template section of this chapter for guidance. In that section there are templates given for a general invocation and specific applications for each one of the steps in the protocol.

For example, invoke to open session, then invoke to cut cords, then invoke to clear the field, et cetera.

Take as much or as little time as you like. The focus of this exercise is to practice creating invocations for specific circumstances and to experience having a tool for anything that comes up in a session.

Notice how it feels to work this way. Notice what words and feelings seem most effective. Notice if you feel doubts. Notice if you feel energy shift. Notice what is working for you and what you are unsure about.

It's all great practice no matter what the results appear to be, so I invite you to keep it light and stay curious.

## The garden of the mind

your consciousness
gives life

to what is planted
in its light

to cultivate thoughts
healing or harmful

nurturing, poisonous
it is your choice

choose well

what you let grow
what you cut down

what kind of harvest
you'd like to receive

the feeling of the fruit
is reflected in its seed

# CHAPTER 6:
# SCANNING ENERGIES +
# CORD CUTTING

*You can't release something you hold in judgment*

## SENSING SUBTLE ENERGIES

One of the most valuable tools you have as a lightworker is the ability to sense and differentiate energies.

The great news for highly sensitive people is that your sensitivity is a powerful asset in discerning subtle energies. Not only that, but when you employ it in this work it can be used as a tool to help free you from the limitations or weaknesses that such sensitivity seems to cause.

What if what you judged as a weakness was actually your superpower?

Whether you consider yourself highly sensitive or are consciously aware of subtle energies or not, your body is certainly aware of them. So if you are unsure, you can allow your body to tell you what it's sensing. Your body is hard-wired to do this, so you need merely re-establish communication with it and you will be able to receive its messages clearly.

How do you open to receive the body's messages? As always, through your intention or willingness. If you are willing to practice the tools of this chapter, you will not only be able to receive, but also to interpret the unique language of your body and your intuition. As you act on the information you receive, you will get the experience of having things confirmed, which eventually builds trust in yourself, your body, and your ability to read energies accurately.

For beginners, the struggle with doubt or confusion can feel intense, but remember that you are not the one doing the work. And when I say you, I mean you as separate from the universe, because whenever you doubt yourself or are struggling to figure something out, you are definitely in the separation/ego mindstate.

The unified mind already knows everything. Therefore, if you think you don't know, you must be identified with the separate—and therefore disempowered—ego mind. If that's the case, the most helpful thing you can do is pause, take a breath, and remember that you as the separate-self are not the one doing the work. You can remind yourself to shift to the unified mindstate and identify as one with the infinite mind in which all things are known.

Whenever you are struggling with scanning, getting an accurate read on an energy, or anything else for that matter, I invite you to release whatever the block is through invocation. Trust that source energy is working through you and that when you're one with the one, you'll get it done. The following story illustrates the power of working with invocation when you sense a weird or unknown energy.

One day I was volunteering in the Pranic Healing clinic where I first trained as a healer. By that time, I had a lot of classes, sessions, and daily practice under my belt and was confident in my skills. I had even been entrusted with helping to run the clinic in my teacher's absence.

That day, while I was working with a client, I saw there was an entity to clear, so I cleared it, but it seemed to come back again and again. I had assumed it was the same one coming back because, based on what I was taught, I thought people would only have one or two entity attachments, if any. Because of my assumption, I was beginning to get a little unsure of my ability to clear the one I was encountering. I started to wonder what was wrong with me. I had always been able to clear entities easily before.

When I stopped assuming and tuned in to what was actually happening, I sensed that it wasn't one entity. It was hundreds, maybe thousands. I saw a huge line of them stretching out beyond the horizon. I realized that the tool I had been using up to that point was completely inadequate. There was a split second of panic, but then I remembered that I wasn't alone. I could pray for help. So I took a deep breath and silently called on infinite source intelligence and all the angelic beings and teachers I could muster to clear whatever it was I was seeing. I put my total conviction into trusting it to be done and gave thanks accordingly.

I was almost scared to scan again to see if the countless entities had cleared, but I had to be sure. I took another deep breath and asked to be shown the truth as I scanned again. To my relief, the entities had cleared. I had tears of gratitude in my eyes as I opened them to see that the energy in the client and the room had shifted.

Here are some of the important points illustrated in the story:

- Stay open to alternate possibilities.
- Don't jump to a conclusion. Rather, ask a question.
- Trust what you sense through your intuition.
- Trust that you have help dealing with whatever it is.

We don't have to be afraid of sensing what is really happening, because no matter what we can handle it. We have access to consciousness and abilities beyond the comprehension of our logical minds and our linear experiences.

Trust that spirit's got your back.

## WAYS OF SENSING ENERGIES

You already know several ways of sensing energies and probably have at least one you use regularly, even if you aren't consciously aware of it. Have you ever:

- Felt the energy in a room shift when someone in a bad mood enters?
- Walked into a building that felt creepy for some reason?
- Thought about calling someone and at the same time they called you?
- Known something, but couldn't explain how you knew it?
- Felt an urge to go a certain way, or heard a voice or a thought in your mind giving you direction that turned out to be helpful?
- Seen something out of the corner of your eye, but when you turned to look at it there was nothing there?
- Felt someone was very sad or upset even though they were acting normal?
- Seen light or lack of light in someone's eyes?
- Felt there was something attached to you that you couldn't seem to shake?

These are examples of sensing subtle energies, and they are all perfectly natural. What is not natural is the way we dismiss what we know. The way the current mainstream culture typically treats this kind of awareness as either special or insignificant. The way that we are told as small children that what we perceive isn't real. The way we are encouraged throughout our lives to repress a significant portion of our awareness.

Because of this kind of social conditioning, we must often relearn the skills we naturally had as children. It takes a bit of practice to deprogram ourselves from our conditioning so that we can access our abilities once again, but since the goal is our natural state of being, the return to it is guaranteed to be successful.

As you practice sensing energies, you will find that some ways come more easily than others. For example, some people are naturally very good at seeing energies, some are better at feeling them. Below is a list of some of the ways people sense subtle energies and the characteristics of having those abilities. As you go through the list, notice which ones you may have experienced before and which seem new to you. Note that the examples given indicate some typical attributes of a particular energy-sensing skill, but you need not have experienced all – or even most – of them to have that skill.

- **Visual/Clairvoyance:** You see energy fields around people or things, you see spirit entities and beings, you see things appear and disappear out of thin air, you see colors or light in or around people, you see pictures in your mind's eye, you can visualize clearly and easily, you have a great sense of direction, you are sensitive to visual stimuli and are very attuned to beauty, art, and decor.

- **Sensual/Clairsentience:** You get gut feelings, you empathically feel other people's emotions or pain in your body, you feel pressure/temperature changes seemingly unrelated to external environment, you get a tingling sensation or chills when something feels true, you're very sensitive to your environment, you find crowds overwhelming, you relate to other people easily, you feel nauseous around violence or dark energies, you have a keen sense of touch/smell/taste, you can feel your moods easily shift to match others and you prefer to be around people who are calm and positive.

- **Aural/Clairaudience:** You hear voices, tones, or frequencies that appear to be external or internal, you hear other people's thoughts, you get messages in spoken forms, you think you hear someone saying something to you when no one is there, you hear things in your mind constantly, you talk to yourself often, you are very sensitive to sounds and prefer quiet time daily.

- **Mental/Claircognizance:** You know something with no explanation, you get a download of information about something all at once, you know the story of something without being told, you're really good at problem solving, when asked a question you know the answer without knowing how you know, you are good at "guessing" things, you can easily learn new things, you are the person people come to for answers, your mind is always going and you find non-mental activities to be relaxing.

Have you experienced or witnessed some of those phenomena? Which ways of sensing subtle energy come more naturally to you? Were you surprised to discover how natural some of these psychic skills are?

As we go through this section on sensing and scanning energies, some techniques might seem impossible for you to do, as though you are being asked to feel things with your hands and you don't have any hands. The wonderful thing about this work is that no matter what your circumstances, you can find a work-around. There are all kinds of creative ways to work with the light of our consciousness and the energy of our bodies.

By the way, did you know that if a physical part of your body is damaged or missing, that part is still intact in your light body or your etheric body? Not only that, but you can actually feel things in your light body as if it were the physical body. If you have the awareness that the energetic blueprint of the light body holds this energy, space, and consciousness, there are many interesting applications.

For example, I might be sitting and talking to a client during an intake and I notice a big cord attached to something they are talking about. It would be distracting for me to start waving my physical hands around to cut it, so I simply visualize my light hands doing it and it works. Another example is I may be holding someone with my physical hands in a biodynamic craniosacral or Reiki hold, and I sense there is a huge heart healing happening, but it would be disruptive for me to move my hands from the hold I'm in, so I imagine that my light hands are holding the heart.

I've also worked with the light body of the client in addition to—or in place of—the physical body. If a woman has had a hysterectomy, I can still work on the uterus in the light body and clear any energetic imprinting there that is causing pain.

Whenever I have done one of these light body or visualization techniques, not only do I feel it, but clients report feeling it, too. I've had people tell me that it felt like there were multiple pairs of hands holding them or that they felt that part of the their body held by or wrapped in light.

That being said, all of the manual or physical techniques are optional anyway, because the primary force we are working with is consciousness. Everything we are doing is at the level of the mind. However, since we are typically identified with the body, the physical experience can be a powerful means to further anchor our intention.

Therefore, whenever you hit a wall and it feels like you are unable to perform a specific lightworking task, you have options:
- Skip it: we're all already perfect anyway.
- Replace it: use another tool instead.
- Imagine it: do it in your mind.

- Invoke it: use three-part prayer power to move the energy.
- Create it: make up your own way of working the tool.
- Surrender it: hand it over to spirit and watch it go.

## ASK YOUR BODY

Did you know that you can ask your body for information? That you can ask it questions and it will answer you? Asking my body is a tool I use continuously in session work and dozens of times throughout the day in my personal life.

Like all animals, the body doesn't lie. Unlike the mind aligned with the ego. Unlike our social conditioning. We can trust it to tell us the truth.

Recall that your body has an amazing capacity to know things. It has an intricate intelligence gathering system you can access. All you need do is ask. Here's how to do it:

**1.** Stand up with your feet close together. When you first start using this tool, it is helpful to have a high center of gravity with a small base, so that when your body weight shifts, you can easily feel it. Eventually you can do it sitting or even lying down.
**2.** Ask your body to give you a "yes" by saying silently or aloud, "Body, show me a yes."
**3.** Notice which way your body sways, moves, or shifts. Thank your body for showing you a "yes."
**4.** Come back to neutral.
**5.** Ask your body for a "no" by saying silently or aloud, "Body, show me a no."
**6.** Notice which way your body sways. Thank your body for showing you a "no."

Now that your body has shown you a "yes" and a "no," practice asking it questions. Start with something small. Ask your body if it would like to drink more water. See what it says.

In **Chapter 4: Development of Intuition**, we learned that when discerning intuitive information, it's either positive, negative, or neutral. It's the same with asking your body. When you ask yes/no questions, you receive either a positive, negative, or neutral answer. If you feel like you're not getting any response, try asking your body if the answer is neutral. If the body says "yes," then you know it's neutral.

I recommend practicing the tool of asking your body every day and starting with things that directly concern the body, like the food it eats and the clothes it wears. Yep, that's right. You are not the one that has to eat or wear that stuff, the body does. Have you ever asked what it wanted?

Try it now with something you have handy. Ask your body, "Do you want to eat this?" "Do you want to wear this?" "What about this?" See what it says.

Every day your body is changing and its needs are changing. Some days it might love wearing a certain piece of jewelry, or eating a certain kind of vegetable, and then not want it at all the next day. Trust what your body is telling you and follow through on doing what it wants as much as possible. If you have a commitment to go to an appointment, but your body doesn't want to, ask it, "How can we make this easier for you?" And then ask it some yes or no questions.

In this way, you build stronger communication and a healthier relationship with the body. You start to trust each other more. Building this foundation is essential. Once you have that, you will trust your body when you ask it something that may feel more high-stakes or significant to you.

You can use the tool of asking your body as a means of getting confirmation for something you may have picked up on psychically. You can use it as a back-up for any of the other scanning tools we'll be learning in this book.

## PRACTICE SEEING ENERGIES

Did you know that it is quite easy to see subtle energies with your physical eyes? It's a matter of training yourself to see with the rods of your eye's retina instead of the cones. We spend most of our time focused on what can be seen with the cones of the retina, so it takes practice to shift out of that mode.

The cones of the eye's retina are the mechanisms responsible for seeing detail and colors. Without the cones, everything would look fuzzy and colorless. The cones allow us to focus visually. They are right in the center of the retina, so when we are focusing, we develop a kind of tunnel vision using only that small portion of our retina to see. This is helpful for filtering out distractions, but the cones are not sensitive enough to pick up on subtle energies. For that, we need to use the rods.

The rods cover the majority of the retina—everywhere else besides the very center where the cones are—and the rods are so incredibly sensitive they can perceive one photon of light. Using the sensitive rods of the retina, it is possible to see those subtle energies that don't seem to be there when you use the cones, so the key to seeing all this cool stuff is not focusing on it. But how can we see something without trying to look at it?

To see something with the rods of your eyes, allow yourself to space out and relax. Let your gaze be soft and your vision go blurry. When using the rods, you're not looking at something in front of you, but receiving visual data from all around you. This type of vision is described as a "wide soak" because it employs the entirety of the retina to soak up the information instead of focusing on something specific.

You can oftentimes see subtle energies in your peripheral vision, but when you turn to look at them, those energies are imperceptible. That's because of the different abilities of the cones and the rods of your eye's retina. In the periphery of your field of vision, you are seeing with the rods. When you turn to focus on what it is, you are seeing with the cones.

In the following exercises we'll practice the wide soak vision technique of employing the rods to see subtle energies.

## EXERCISE :: CLAIRVOYANCE PRACTICE #1

For this experiment you will need access to a patch of sky to gaze at. You can stand outside or look out the window. It is easier if there is nothing between you and the air, like a pane of glass, so if you are looking out a window, open it. You also need a patch of open sky unobstructed by trees or buildings. Clouds are okay. As a matter of fact, I recommend trying this exercise with different weather conditions to see what changes. In my experience, it is easiest for most people on clear, sunny days; it is moderately easy on overcast days; and most difficult on rainy days. So if you have trouble on a cloudy day, try again on a sunny day.

Once you get your patch of sky, your assignment is to stare into the middle distance and space out. You are not trying to look at anything or see anything specific. You must totally relax your eyes and your forehead. Soften your gaze. Allow your eyes be so soft that the eyelids close slightly like a peaceful Buddha. Allow your face to be soft. Relax into a smile so gentle that it barely moves your lips. Allow everything in your sight to blur and soften. And notice. Is it just empty space you're gazing into? Or is there something else in the emptiness? If you start to focus on what you see and lose it, take a deep breath, relax, and un-focus again.

This is a practice of allowing-versus-striving. Go ahead and try it.

Seriously, try it right now. It will only take a minute and it's super fun. I'll even hold your place here with some dots.

...................................................

What did you find in your experiment? Was it difficult to maintain not-focusing? What did you see? Did you have any other kinds of awareness while you were spacing out?

## EXERCISE :: CLAIRVOYANCE PRACTICE #2

Another practice is gazing at trees. Again, this is easiest to do on a sunny summer day, when the tree's leaves are open and there's a lot of energy in the canopy. You will want to get a patch of sky with a tree, gaze at the area where the edge of the tree's canopy meets the sky, and do the same practice of letting the eyes un-focus and relax. Check it out. Can you see anything around the tree?

## EXERCISE :: CLAIRVOYANCE PRACTICE #3

A similar exercise can be done with a person. This one is easier inside in a room with moderate light and a blank, light-colored, preferably white wall as a background. You can even practice this randomly when you are in different conducive locations with different people. If they aren't people you know, they may feel it is disconcerting for you to be staring at them, so be discrete. The exercise is the same: un-focus the eyes, gaze softly, and notice what you see.

## EXERCISE :: CLAIRVOYANCE PRACTICE #4

You can do a similar exercise on your own at home with your hands. Simply find a blank background, hold your hands up in front of you, arms out-stretched, palms facing toward you, fingers pointing at each other. Un-focus the eyes, relax, gaze at the middle distance, and allow the hands to be blurry. Then slowly move the hands away from each other, and then slowly back again. Keep the eyes soft. See what happens. I'll give you a moment to do it now.

........................................

What did you notice? When you looked with the rods were you able to see things you couldn't see with the cones?

A useful thing about these exercises is that you can see for yourself some of the subtle energies we will be working with throughout this course, but like I've mentioned before, if you have difficulty seeing these things, don't worry. You can still do lightwork, even if you don't see the light.

## EXERCISE :: MANUAL SENSING PRACTICE

Much like how our eyes are equipped with natural mechanisms to see subtle energies, our hands are similarly equipped to feel subtle energies. When you use your hands to sense energy, you may feel a sensation in them or you may get a sense that the hand is picking up on something without you being aware that you are feeling anything physically. Like me, you might experience both.

Let's try an exercise to see if we can sense energies in our hands. First, rub your hands together briskly to wake them up. You can even look at them and tell them, silently or out loud, "wake up" or "activate."

Imagine or feel your hands start to activate and become energized. Then hold the hands up in front of you, palms facing each other, arms and shoulders relaxed, hands awake but relaxed. Next, slowly bring the hands closer together. Notice what you feel. Bring them slowly apart. Notice what you feel. You may wish to close your eyes. Breathe. Slowly move the hands. Notice. Feel into the space between your hands. Take your time.

Go ahead and try it now. It will just take a minute to slow down and feel it.

..............................................

What did you notice? Was it just empty space between your hands or was there something going on there? Did it feel the same coming together and pulling apart, or was it different? Did it feel stronger when your hands were closer together or farther apart?

Try again and see if you notice anything else. Maybe other senses kick in. Try experimenting with different hand positions. Instead of palm-to-palm, try palm-to-fingertip or fingertip-to-fingertip.

## SCANNING FOR SPECIFIC ENERGIES

Now that we have practiced sensing or feeling energy with the hands, let's experiment with a practical application of scanning for specific energies.

For this first exercise, let's practice scanning for the light body I mentioned earlier—and which you may have even seen in clairvoyance exercise 3 or 4 above. The light body, also called the etheric body or the etheric blueprint, is the energetic body most like our physical bodies. It surrounds and interpenetrates the physical body and has all the parts of and information for the physical body, hence the term "blueprint."

The etheric light body is quite dense compared to the other energetic bodies or fields around the physical body, so it is fairly easy to see or sense. In the following practice, we will touch the edge of it with our hands to get an idea of how far out it extends from the physical body.

When scanning for the etheric body manually, it is helpful to scan an area where there isn't a major energy center. A large chakra can be distracting, so choosing an area like the outside of your thigh is perfect.

## EXERCISE :: SCAN THE ETHERIC BODY

**1.** Activate your hands physically by rubbing them together and/or mentally with your intention. You might look at them and say, "Hands, activate."
**2.** Extend your arms out to either side of your body, palms of the hands facing toward your thighs.
**3.** Set an intention to scan for the etheric body. You may think to yourself, "I am scanning for my etheric body" or "Show me the etheric body."
**4.** Slowly bring the hands toward the body. Let the hands stop wherever they stop. You may feel a sensation in your hands like pressure, tingling, or

temperature change. You may feel like you hit an invisible barrier. You may not feel anything, but the hands just stop on their own. Trust your hands. They know what they're doing.

**5.** Notice where the hands stopped. How far does the etheric body extend from the physical body?

**6.** Scan different areas of the body. Stretch the arms wide, set your intention for finding the edge of the etheric body, then bring the hands toward the body till they stop.

**7.** Notice the size of the etheric body in different areas of the physical body.

What did you notice? Was the etheric body bigger in some places than others, or pretty even all around? How did it feel? Did you get any other information besides size? Did different areas feel different somehow? Were some places easier to scan than others?

If you couldn't find the edge of your etheric body, it's very possible that it was beyond the distance your arms could reach. Do you get a sense that this could be true? Either way, it's fine because soon we will learn a tool for scanning energies that are out of your physical reach.

While doing the scanning exercise, did you pick up on additional information about a part of your light body? If feeling is one of the ways you sense subtle energies, this can happen as you touch an energy with your hand. It can be helpful for intuitively guiding your work flow. If you don't notice things like that, don't worry, there are other things that can intuitively guide your session work.

When you first start doing these kinds of energy scans, you may not always get consistent feedback from your hands. It can feel like sometimes it works and sometimes it doesn't. That's totally normal. Like any new skill, with consistent practice comes consistent ability. If you feel confused or stuck, remember to pause, take a breath, invoke, and try again.

As you go through the exercises in this book, remember, it is more helpful to do a few minutes of practice once or twice a day than it is to do a marathon practice once a week, so if you start to get fatigued, distracted, or overwhelmed, take a break and return to the exercise refreshed.

## ETHERIC CORDS

We are going to continue with further practical application of our scanning tool, scanning specifically for etheric cords. But before we do that, let's look at what these energetic cords are and why we might like to clear them.

Etheric cords are an energetic manifestation of our mental attachments and entanglements. These attachments include:

- **Judgments:** everything we've decided is good or bad, right or wrong. "That person is horrible." "That's the best/worst thing ever." "I know I'm right." "I don't want to be wrong."
- **Opinions:** another, more subtle kind of judgment. "That shade of blue is ugly." "This is the best way to make coffee." "Roses are prettier than daisies." "I don't look good in those pants."
- **Stories:** repeated thoughts about the past. "She hurt me." "That guy is always a jerk." "I've never been good at learning languages." "I'm an alcoholic."
- **Meanings:** our interpretation of events. "Doing that means you don't love me." "If you cared you would do this." "It's because there's something wrong with me." "If I could be better it would be different."

All of these things are inventions of our minds. None of them are real, but we believe that they are. At some point we chose to believe them, whether consciously or not. In fact, many of these attachments are not in our conscious awareness, but with practice we can become aware of them. With awareness comes the possibility for more conscious choices.

What makes the energy of attachment so sticky is the unquestioning nature in which we accept these beliefs, construct computations, and draw erroneous conclusions based on their false premises. When we believe in things that we've made up which aren't true, it leads to conflict in our mind. To manage and cope with the conflict, we build cases, gather evidence, and argue for or against our beliefs. We struggle with feelings of injustice and intense mental and emotional suffering. We become upset with the triggering and traumatizing stories and meanings we create. We unnecessarily re-traumatize ourselves over and over with our mental habits of judging, blaming, shaming, and punishing.

It's important for each of us to acknowledge the trauma and conditioning incurred earlier in our lives. Acknowledgement is an important step in
healing. It's also important to acknowledge that we may be operating under
a belief system based on the limits of the past and not on the possibility
available in the present. If we continue to run these trauma-based belief
programs, we will never heal the trauma. If we don't challenge the beliefs of
our conditioning, we will never create something new.

Can we really judge the meaning of things? Take this small example: you're
driving and you miss your turn. You immediately judge it and yourself as
wrong and get upset. You drive around the block and because of that little bit of extra time you now arrive at your destination just as someone is
pulling out of the perfect parking spot for you. Now, is it wrong that you
missed the turn or is it right? Was it good or was it bad?

How many times has something happened that you judged as wrong in
the moment, but later decided that you wouldn't trade for anything in
the world? What if all of our judgments and beliefs don't actually mean
anything?

For years I carried intense shame over things I had done in my life that
I had judged as wrong, like getting addicted to drugs and behaviors or
staying in abusive relationships. I couldn't imagine there being any kind
of silver lining to such painful experiences, but sure enough, I see the val-
ue now. These days, I use that learning from the past to hold a space of
understanding and healing for my clients. Having worked through those
things myself, I can share tools that I know actually work and I have deep
compassion for what other people are going through. It's weird to say I'm
grateful for those things, especially if I'm having a moment of feeling my
past trauma being triggered, but I can at least say that I took that shit and
turned it into alchemical gold.

What if there is some beauty that can be created from your painful past?
Would you be open to it? Would you be willing to release your judgments,
stories and meanings of the past to transmute the energy into something

greater than you ever imagined?

If the answer is yes, take a breath with me now and let it be.

And remember, releasing judgment does not mean condoning harmful behavior. It means disentangling yourself from the energy of the harmfulness so that you can be free.

**FREEDOM AS A WAY OF LIFE**

Would you like to experience life without the huge energy drain of countless etheric cords of attachment? If so, I have great news for you. If you practice the mindset of non-judgment you will accumulate fewer and fewer cords and eventually be free of them.

Freedom requires great willingness and practice, but even after a short amount of investment you will notice a difference in your energy. You will also notice that without the energetic entanglement of cords it is far easier to change things you'd like to change. The key to staying cord-free is to continually release all of your judgments and the meaning you've made of everything.

**The world isn't meaningless, but your made-up meanings about it are.**

As we go about our day-to-day lives, we get countless opportunities to remind ourselves to practice non-judgment. When we notice a judgment arise in our mind, sometimes we can clear the energy just by being aware of it as something that is not real. But what if it doesn't clear right away?

You've already learned a tool to deal with anything that arises in the energy. It's invocation. Try an invocation with the intention of "I am grateful to be clearing any and all judgments, opinions, stories and meaning that I've made now." Or you can invoke to, "Clear all cords now."

The simple consciousness tools of awareness and intent can clear your judgments any time you feel upset. When you're upset, it is always about the

underlying energy of your judgment, story, or meaning about what is happening, not the thing itself. As we've learned, most of these attachments
are based on unresolved trauma that is getting triggered. It is far kinder to
yourself to clear the underlying energy all the way back to the root cause to
free yourself of suffering than it is to focus on the apparent cause of upset
in the world of form.

I am not saying that it is wrong to get upset. Getting upset is normal. What
I am saying is that holding on to upsetting energy is harmful for your body.
Things happen. That's neutral. Holding onto judgments about those things
is what gives them an energetic charge, either negative or positive. Your
body is the one who will get hit with that energy. Your body responds to
your every thought and feeling.

When we hold a space of non-judgment, we are doing it for ourselves, to
heal ourselves, because we love ourselves. We are not doing it for anyone
else, although it does have the power to heal everyone, because we are one.

In the moment of upset, it is often very challenging to find the willingness
to let go of the underlying judgment, but the sooner you clear the upsetting
belief, the sooner you will relieve yourself of toxic energy drains that sap
your life force energy and make you more susceptible to illness and distress.
Think of it this way: whatever is arising, you will be infinitely better-suited
to deal with it if you aren't getting upset and drained by your attachments.

Sometimes we judge ourselves for having judgments. How helpful do you
suppose that is? I've been there and done that so many times. What a ham-
ster wheel of suffering that is. I am reminding all of us that we have been
immersed in these belief systems for ages. We hold them on different levels
of our being. Some of them are inherited, some multidimensional. Wherever or whatever their origins are, judging ourselves for having limiting
beliefs and judgments doesn't help them clear any faster.

We don't need to judge anything we're clearing and we don't need to figure
it all out either. In fact, needing to figure something out before you can let
it go can be an ego trap. It is more helpful to think, "I don't know why/
where/how I have these judgments, but I know I am clearing them all now."

In fact saying, "I don't know" is one of the most powerful ways I know of to clear the energy of attachment.

This tool has really helped me a lot. I've learned that when we are in our pain and judgment we are identified with the aspect of our mind that doesn't know, so acknowledging that starts to shift the energy. I've been able to stop myself from thinking things like, "You're so fucked up for staying with that psychopath," and instead, I've started to say things like, "I don't know why I stayed in that abusive relationship."

Like I said, non-judgment doesn't mean condoning behaviors that are antisocial, toxic, or harmful. True non-judgment allows us to be more empowered to act strongly and decisively. We won't be spending energy and time caught up in our mental/emotional reactions or resistance to what is. We will see and know clearly what is happening in the moment. With that clarity and presence, we will act to help ourselves without distraction.

## ARE THERE GOOD CORDS?

I used to worry about being right all the time. I wanted to make sure I believed in the right thing. I wanted to make sure I did healing practices the right way. When I cut cords, I didn't want to cut the wrong cords. I wanted to keep the good cords and get rid of the bad. That was before I understood that the energies of what we've judged as good or bad is what cords are.

Originally, I was taught that there are good and bad cords. I was taught to have an intention to scan for only "unauthorized and inappropriate" cords, but the more I got curious and experimented, I saw that all cords were keeping us entangled with our old baggage.

Here's what I learned about cords:
• All of our judgments, cravings, and aversions take the form of energetic cords that bind and limit us.
• All cords and attachments are an unnecessary energy drain and maybe even the cause of all human suffering.
• No judgment or belief in right or wrong or good or bad is necessary,

because the truth will still be the truth no matter what we believe.

When I realized that I didn't have to believe in anything, I felt an almost ecstatic sense of relief. That ecstasy and lightness was my freedom and power returning, because all beliefs are artificial constructs and all cords are energy drains.

**It takes a lot of energy to maintain the appearance of a seemingly real invention.**

How much energy and power could you reclaim by releasing all your beliefs?

The truth is the truth and doesn't require anyone's belief in it. It will make itself evident to anyone who clears the clutter of their own interpretations. Therefore, it is infinitely more powerful to release all beliefs and judgments and simply be open to knowing the truth.

So, when I'm cutting cords or releasing attachments, I'm not interested in keeping any of them. Cords are an energetic manifestation of mental attachments. Attachments cause suffering, conflict, and confusion.

But are there good attachments? Students frequently ask me, "What about good attachment? Like, attachment to my child? I don't want to cut something that shouldn't be cut."

My response to that is: don't worry. You can't destroy a love bond. You can't destroy connection. Our human inventions of attachment are not the same as organic connection. Our connection to everyone and everything in the oneness of life is eternal. Love is eternal.

Have you ever still loved someone regardless of how bad things got in your relationship? Have you ever loved someone even though you didn't agree with their actions or lifestyle? Have you ever loved this world even though it is rife with suffering, trauma, and insane human inventions?

Love is a force of nature. Love is a universal law. Love is the energy that creates and sustains the universe. We can't destroy love. We can believe we can, though. We can believe in all kinds of nonsense, which is exactly the kind of thing this course is designed to help clear.

## CUTTING CORDS ON THE BIOFIELD LEVEL

We've defined cords as attachments and we have clarified the appropriateness of cutting or releasing all of them. So now we get to the fun part: practice.

For this exercise we will be using a similar technique to scanning for the etheric body, but this time we will be scanning for cords anywhere on or in the body's biofield or aura, which is the electromagnetic field of energy around the physical body.

Remember that any time you engage in lightwork, your light body hands will activate and you will be using light fingers that are much larger than your physical hands. You will also be directing subtle energy through your intention, so remember not to view things through a literal/physical lens, but rather see them as symbolic gestures. Just as these words I'm writing are symbols of the thoughts about the experiences I wish to share with you and not the actual experiences themselves, these tools we are working with are the symbolic language of lightwork.

## EXERCISE :: CUTTING CORDS :: PART 1

**1.** Take a deep breath, get present, and invoke.
**2.** Activate your light hands by rubbing your physical hands together.
**3.** Set an intention to scan the whole front side of your biofield for cords.
**4.** Begin by stretching your arms out, right arm reaching up and left one reaching down, a bit in front of your body, with the palms of the hands facing each other.
**5.** Next, slowly bring your hands toward each other with the intention of scanning for cords. (Remember, if you don't have a strong intention, you could be picking up on all sorts of different energies.) You might think,

"Show me the cords."

**6.** As you slowly scan through the biofield, allow the hands to stop wherever you feel something (tingling, pressure, temperature) or wherever the hands just stop on their own (without any sensation) or wherever you get an intuitive idea of stopping. That is where the cords are. Don't think about it. Trust it.

**7.** Condense all the cords you found by pushing them down with the right hand into the left hand.

**8.** Grab a hold of the condensed cords with the left hand, and pull them away from your body.

**9**. With the light fingers of your free right hand acting as the blade, make a cutting or chopping motion between the left hand and your body and cut through those cords three times: chop chop chop!

**10.** With the left hand that's holding the cords, take the ends of the cut cords and imagine you are plugging them into the Earth (thank you, Earth!) and release.

**11.** Repeat the process. Scan again to see if there are more cords, following the steps below. It usually takes a few passes to clear all the cords. Sometimes several passes when you first start. Everyone is different. Trust it is working.

**12.** Reach the hands out again, bring the hands toward each other with the intention of scanning for cords, allow the hands to stop wherever they stop. That's where the cords are now. Are there less this time? Gather up all the cords in your left hand, pull them out, chop chop chop, plug into the earth and release.

**13.** Scan again. If there are still cords, go through the process again: gathering, pulling, cutting, releasing, and scanning again until the hands don't hit anything because there are no cords to scan.

**14.** Give thanks. Clear your hands with an invocation.

Note that when cord cutting, it is more effective for permanent release to plug them into an alternate energy source. I have found through practice with myself, clients, and students that the Earth seems to be the easiest energy source for folks to use. That being said, I was originally taught to give them to an angel or plug them into a prayer, so there are definitely other effective ways. I suggest starting with the Earth and if that doesn't work for you, experiment to find something that does.

Now that there are no more cords on the front of your field, it's time to scan for cords on the back.

## EXERCISE :: CUTTING CORDS :: PART 2

It is pretty awkward to scan your own back the way we did the front, so for the back we will practice a modification of the technique and imagine that we are standing behind ourselves.

**1.** Invoke.
**2.** Imagine you are looking at your own back. It's okay if you don't visualize it. An intention is enough.
**3.** Extend your arms, right one up, left one down, palms facing each other.
**4.** State in your mind an intention to scan for any cords on your back, then bring the hands towards each other with the right hand moving down and the left one moving up. Wherever you feel the hands stop, that's where the cords are.
**5.** Gather the cords into your left hand and pull them away from your imagined back (towards you), then use the right hand to cut the cords between your left hand and your back (chop chop chop), and use the left hand to plug the cords into the Earth to release them.
**6.** Scan again, gather, chop, release and repeat until all cords on the back have been released.
**7.** Give thanks.

Congratulations, not only did you just complete a manual cord cutting, but you also employed a remote healing technique to do it.

Remote healing simply means that rather than working on something in real time-space, the work is done at a distance of time, space, or both. This technique, which is accomplished merely through your willingness, intention, and imagination, can be used with great success any time you'd like to work on an area in time or space that is difficult – or just inconvenient – to reach physically.

For example, we can use it in this next exercise, cutting cords on specific, localized areas, like chakras or tissues of the body.

## CUTTING CORDS IN SPECIFIC AREAS

Now that we have gone through a generalized clearing of whatever cords are in our bodies' electromagnetic biofields or auras, we can get more specific and do localized cord cutting. For this exercise, we will be looking for cords in chakras, but the same technique can be used for removing cords from other specific things, such as tissues of the physical body, thought forms, people, or situations.

For now, let's start with scanning in real time-space on the front of our solar plexus chakra, then switch to remote healing for the back. The solar plexus is a major energy center at the diaphragm, or between the heart and navel. We'll be exploring the major centers of the body when we get to Chapter 8, but you don't have to know anything about the centers to scan them for cords, or anything else for that matter. If you'd like a visual guide, you can look at the Chakra Chart in the Appendix.

## EXERCISE :: CUTTING CORDS ON A CHAKRA

**1.** Invoke.
**2.** Assume the scanning position: right hand up, left hand down, palms facing each other, and position the hands above and below the area of the solar plexus.
**3.** Set an intention of scanning for cords in the solar plexus. Wherever the hands stop, that's where the cords are. (If you don't get any cords here, try a different area of the body or chakra for practice.)
**4.** Gather the cords into your left hand, pull them away from your solar plexus, or other chakra, and chop chop chop with the right hand.
**5.** Plug the cords into the Earth with your left hand and release.
**6.** Scan again, repeating the process until all cords have been cleared from the front solar plexus, or whatever chakra you're working on.
**7.** Give thanks.

For the back side of the chakra, let's practice the remote technique:

**1.** Invoke.
**2.** Imagine that the back solar plexus area is conveniently right in front of you. (You don't have to know what it looks like. Intention is all that is needed.)
**3.** Bring the hands to the cord scanning position at the top and bottom of the back solar plexus.
**4.** Set an intention to scan for cords on the back solar plexus chakra and scan, bringing the hands towards each other until they stop. (If you don't pick up any cords here, try a different area on your back)
**5.** Gather the cords into the left hand, pull them out of the back solar plexus (toward you) chop with the right hand, plug into the Earth and release.
**6.** Scan again and repeat until clear.
**7.** Give thanks.

Note that you can use the remote technique for anything. We've been using it to work on our backs, but you can scan any chakra remotely and, in fact, this is how we can work on anyone or anything, anywhere in the world. How cool is that?

For practice, scan all the major chakras for cords and try both on-the-body and remote cord cutting. Practice the general application on the overall biofield and localized application on specific chakras and areas of the body.

## APPLICATIONS FOR CORD CUTTING

Cord cutting can be used as a stand-alone tool or as a part of a larger session. In the Lightworker Session Protocol it is used after initial invocation and before clearing. If you cut cords before clearing, your clearing work will go much faster.

Cord cutting is also employed at the end of a session to release the energy and clear attachment to the outcome of the work. Even if you are working on yourself, it is helpful to release the energy and clear the attachment to the outcome, maybe even more so.

Cord cutting can also be used in the moment as a tool to release attachments. In a moment of emotional upset, you can use it to clear the underlying judgment. You can use it to clear the energy of craving or aversion when you are obsessing over something.

If there is someone, something, or someplace that you'd like to stop sending energy to, you can cut the cord. Say there's an unloving thought in your awareness. You can scan for the cord between you and that thought form and cut it.

See what kinds of application possibilities arise for you and bring them into your practice. These tools are here to assist you in cultivating the kinds of empowering thoughts that will nourish you in daily life. Take time each day to tend to the garden of your mind.

## CHAPTER 6 :: KEY POINTS

- Everyone has the natural ability to sense energy in their own way.
- Everyone can practice cultivating psychic skills.
- You can choose the thoughts you'd like to cultivate.
- If you find a thought in your mind that you don't enjoy the effects of, you can weed it out.
- Our ideas about things can block us from seeing the truth.
- The judgments, meaning, and stories we make up are attachments.
- Our attachments manifest in the subtle energetic realms as etheric cords.
- Etheric cords will prevent energy from clearing.
- Etheric cords of attachment can be released.
- Cutting cords releases attachment to outcomes, people, situations, or any other kind of energy.
- We can stop accumulating cords by staying in a mindstate of non-judgment.

## CHAPTER 6 :: INTEGRATION TIPS

- Cut cords every night before bed. Notice the quality of your sleep.

• Any time you find yourself judging something, cut the cords of attachment.

• Any time you are having trouble scanning or clearing something, cut the cords of attachment.

• Any time you are feeling crappy about yourself, scan to see how many cords of judgment are there. Do you really want those?

• When you are working to release an old pattern, check to see if there are any cords of attachment to doing the "right" thing or the "wrong" thing. Sometimes what we've judged as right can be even more limiting than what we've judged as wrong.


## CHAPTER 6 :: PRACTICUM POSSIBILITIES

**Scan Auras with a Friend:** (about 10 minutes)

If you have a friend who likes playing with energy, try this fun exercise. First, get a baseline scan of where your friend's etheric body is today. Next, experiment with having your friend hold a crystal and scan the field again. What happened?

Try having your friend hold different kinds of food, or thinking different kinds of thoughts. Scan each time to see how the energy of the item or thought affects the size of the field. What kinds of things make the etheric body bigger? What kinds of things make it smaller?

**Develop a Cord Cutting System:** (about 10 minutes)

When going through the major chakras scanning for and cutting cords, practice working with a system so that as you are doing the work you can spend less time and energy figuring out where you are in the process. Use the Chakra Chart in the Appendix for reference if needed. Here are some examples of patterns you may choose:

• Loop up the back, down the front: start at the bottom of the back, work up the back to the crown, then work the front side from the top down;

• Loop up the front, down the back: start on the front at the bottom, work up to the crown and then down the back from top to bottom;
• Loop from the crown: start either a back-to-front loop or front-to-back loop starting at the top of the body instead of the bottom;
• Spiral up: start at the bottom and do both front and back of the first chakra, then front and back of the second chakra, then the third, then the fourth, et cetera until you reach the top; or
• Spiral down: same as above, but working from the top down.

See which one of these patterns feels most intuitive for you. Pick one with which to work and try sticking to that system. Having some built-in patterns and structure can be a time-saving strategy for your practice. It is especially helpful when you are following the energy on some intuitive tangent and you want to remember where you left off.

**Creative Cord Cutting:** (in the moment)

Some time when you are practicing cutting cords, try mixing up your technique with one of these variations:

• Imagine you are giving the cords to source energy.
• Imagine that you are pulling the cords out completely by the root instead of chopping them.
• Imagine that instead of pulling or cutting the cords, you are infusing them with a brilliant white light that completely dissolves them.

What technique felt most powerful for you? Can you sense that some variations might be more effective than others in certain circumstances?

**Fields of creation**


breathe kindness
in this sacred space

inhabit the still point
balanced between

inhale
and
exhale

luxuriate
in the suspension
of opposition

revel in the beauty
of eternal moments

choosing you
and all of you

to bask in the truth
of holy relation

to feel the embrace
of all creation

you enter
this temple of presence
with reverence

and vigilance
only for love

# CHAPTER 7:
# ENERGY CLEARING + THE BIOFIELD

*Heal yourself, heal the world*

## ENERGY CLEARING

So far in this course we've learned how to use the power of our mind, connect with source energy, work with intentions, sense or scan energies, and clear the entanglements of our judgments. Now we are ready for learning about clearing the gunk out of our fields.

We've already practiced clearing energies through prayer or invocation, but there are as many ways of clearing energies as you can imagine.

The following are some ways of clearing energetic congestion from bodies, spaces, fields, or properties. Most of them are free and many you already know:

• **Sound**: Tones, chants, bells, singing bowls, songs, snapping/clapping, rattles, drums.
• **Plants**: Smudge, herbal mist or spray, herb brushing, incense, aromatherapy, eating/being with greens/herbs.
• **Water**: Baptism, ritual baths, showering, being in or near rivers/oceans,

drinking water.
- **Minerals**: Salt, selenite, green crystals, mineral/salt baths.
- **Earth**: Lying on the ground, burying in earth, feeling connected to the Earth.
- **Sunlight**: Bathing in the sunlight, allowing sunlight into a space.
- **Fire**: Ritual burning of offerings, cooking out impurities, visualizing fire.
- **Air**: Circulating fresh air, airing something out, breathing.
- **Movement**: Dancing, stretching, shaking, tapping, massaging.
- **Meditation**: Awareness and allowance, undoing by not-doing.
- **Visualization**: Imagination, psychic structures.
- **Intention**: Mental techniques, invocation, prayer.
- **Light**: Using the light of spirit/consciousness, our light.

Isn't the abundance of our resources amazing? Energetic support is all around us. It is literally in the air we breathe. We can consciously tap into the healing power of nature any time, regardless of our circumstances.

For the upcoming exercise on clearing the body's biofield later in this chapter, we'll be focusing on a manual sweeping technique. It is a tool that combines three ways of clearing energy: intention, light, and movement.

Manual sweeping techniques in energy work are somewhat similar to physical bodywork techniques. Just like a massage therapist can detect a tightness in a muscle and help release it, so can an energy worker detect congestion in the energy body and help release it. And just like it is helpful for body workers to understand physical anatomy, it is helpful for lightworkers to understand energetic anatomy.

There are similarities in physical and energetic anatomy. In physical anatomy you can focus on the cellular level, the individual organs, or the larger body systems. The same is true with energetic anatomy. You can focus on tissues or organs, parts of chakras, whole chakra fields, the overall biofield of the entire body, or the rays of light that extend through the fields.

In session work, you may not have time to address all the levels involved in a particular healing, and that's okay. Whatever level you work at is perfect. I have found for the sake of efficiency, it is helpful to start a clearing with the overall biofield or auric field of the body, because it will affect all the other fields within it.

## THE HUMAN BIOFIELD

The human electromagnetic energy field is your body's personal atmosphere. Also known as the biofield or aura, It is the field of energy that supports and surrounds the body. The biofield affects the chakral, mental, emotional, and physical bodies within it, and they affect it. It is the energy your many bodies are working in, breathing in, and soaking in.

If your biofield is clear and strong, it will support your many-bodied self in feeling clear and strong. If the biofield is congested with heavy energy, thought forms, and entities, it will affect the vitality and peace of the bodies within it. If the biofield is weak, you could experience energy leaks and lack of healthy boundaries. You could soak up other people's energies or attract energy vampires.

Keeping your biofield clear is tremendously helpful to overall health and wellness and it is the first in a series of energy clearing techniques we will learn. Before getting into specifics of how to clear the biofield, let's look at the structure of this field and the fields within it.

## TOROIDAL FIELDS

The electromagnetic field of the body and the smaller fields within that field—like the chakra centers—are toroidal fields. Toroidal fields are energy dynamics that run in a geometric shape called a torus. A torus is shaped similarly to a doughnut. It is a continuous surface with a hole in the middle.

In the case of our body's biofield, the doughnut shape is more like an apple. And the hole in the middle is tighter, like a core. Also like an apple, the biofield of our bodies has dimples—or vortices—of energy at both the top and the bottom. This kind of apple-shaped torus is called a horn torus.

Toroidal fields are found everywhere in nature and are made of the stuff that surrounds them, like a whirlpool is made of water and a tornado is made of air. The toroidal fields of people are made of the energy and light that we are.

We have toroidal fields in the smallest bits of matter, like atoms and cells, all the way up to the largest bodies, such as planets, stars, galaxies and the cosmos itself. We are all fields within fields within fields. Each one of these fields has its own consciousness and is distinct unto itself, and yet is simultaneously connected to every other field in the web of life.

The energy dynamic of a toroidal field is naturally self-sustaining and balancing. By remembering this pattern we naturally come into alignment with that sustenance and balance. Just by thinking of the fields, meditating on the torus, or intending to activate it, we can help to energize and balance our biofields and chakra fields, have stronger boundaries, and leak less energy.

As you read the following descriptions of toroidal fields, see if you can release the need to visualize them perfectly or figure them out exactly. I invite you to open to the possibility that just by being in a state of wondering about them, you are strengthening your fields and your awareness of them.

Toroidal fields are actually a *double* torus, two tori overlapping each other. The overlapping tori create a strong field through the balance of the opposing forces of energy.

In the toroidal field, energy circulates from outside to inside and from inside to outside in a continuous flow. It is also moving both up and down—or front to back—simultaneously. In the case of the overall biofield pattern that surrounds the body, there is a torus moving from crown to root and an opposing torus moving energy from root to crown. Let's look a bit closer at how these energy dynamics work.

Imagine there is a field of energy shaped like an apple. In this field, energy is moving up the skin—or outside—of the apple. As it gets to the top, if the energy keeps going, it will move toward the dimple—or vortex—at the center. When the energy gets to that dimple, it gets sucked down into

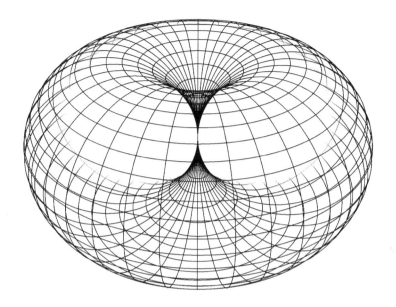

*Example of toroidal field*

the core. It goes down the channel of the core and exits the dimple at the bottom. If it keeps moving, it will move out toward the edge of the apple and start moving up the outside again toward the top. Can you get a sense of how this cycle looks?

Now imagine that the energy moving around the apple field is also cycling down the outside of the skin. So this opposing field dynamic of the apple is moving energy down the outside edge. It gets to the bottom and if it keeps moving, it will enter into the lower dimple/vortex. From there, it moves up the core till it gets to the top. At the top, it exits out the upper dimple/vortex. If it keeps moving, it will go all the way to the edge and cascade back down the outside to the bottom of the field.

Remember that as energy is circulating through these toroidal fields it is spiraling. It spirals as it moves up and down and it spirals as it moves in and out.

Imagine a spiraling vortex of energy at your crown. It's pulling in energy.

This energy is spiraling down into the central core in the middle of your body. The energy continues to spiral down and out the root vortex at your perineum. The root vortex spirals it down and out to the edge of the field. From there, the energy spirals back up the outside of the field to the top, where it gets sucked back into the crown vortex again.

Simultaneously, there is another torus that is spiraling energy in the opposite direction. This energy is spiraling down the outside of the field, getting sucked in and up into the root vortex, up the core, and out the crown and back out to the edge where it spirals down again.

It can be difficult to visualize—or even wrap your mind around—these complex energy dynamics, so don't worry if you feel a bit confused. If you

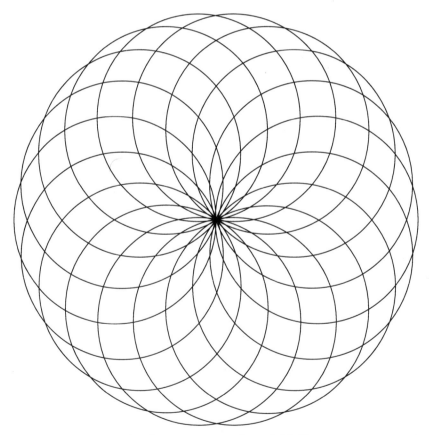

*Overlapping vortices of toroidal field*

feel attached to figuring it out, check to see if there is a cord to cut.

When the double torus is viewed from the angle of looking into the spiraling vortices of the overlapping tori, as shown on the facing page, it displays the pattern of the phi-ratio double spiral. This pattern creates a natural density around the outer edge, which acts as an energetic boundary. When our fields are strong, we have a natural boundary that allows our bodies to feel more at home in their own space and less likely to absorb external energies or to leak energy.

For a fun practice, use the illustrations in this chapter or search online for images of toroidal fields. Look at the images and imagine them around and within your body. Many images will only show the spiral of one torus, but in your imagination you can practice spiraling the energy both ways, top to bottom and bottom to top.

You may even start to have an awareness that one direction feels stronger or that your field feels a little lop-sided. Just noticing this will start to shift the energy if you allow it to shift. It's truly amazing what happens when we get present and become aware of what is happening.

In subsequent chapters we will look at ways of balancing fields, but for now we will focus on clearing, because oftentimes just clearing the field will allow it to balance and strengthen on its own.

## CLEARING TOROIDAL FIELDS

If we are aware of the structure or dynamics of the electromagnetic fields of our bodies, it will be easier to move energy through or out of them. We can go with the flow and it will make our work much easier.

Therefore, when clearing a field, it is helpful to sweep out the congested energy in a way that corresponds to the shape and flow of that energy field or part of the field. For example:

• **Fields**: When clearing the overall sphere of the field, it is easiest to sweep the light hands through it as if tracing longitudinal lines on a globe, with the hands following the curve of the sphere.

• **Vortices**: When clearing the entry/exit vortex of a field, it is fastest to sweep the light hands in a swirling or circular motion, moving from inner to outer.

• **Channels**: When clearing out the central channel or core of the field, it is most effective to sweep the light hands from the top to bottom with the hands following the line or shape of the channel.

In **Chapter 8: Chakra Form + Function + Clearing**, we'll be exploring clearing the vortices and channels of the fields. For now, let's look more closely at the details of clearing the overall sphere of the body's biofield.

## MANUAL SWEEPING

The most common manual technique for clearing energies in this course is called sweeping. It involves running the light hands through the field in a sweeping motion to remove congested or diseased energies, which are then disposed of safely. The sweeping technique layers several tools in one: intention, visualization, light, and movement. Any time techniques are layered, the work is more powerful.

There are other manual techniques that you can employ in clearing energies. Sometimes I simply energize something with light in order to dissolve it. We will look at those techniques more in **Chapter 9: Energizing + Sealing + Harmonizing**.

Since we are reaching into the field with our light hands and sweeping/ pulling energetic congestion out manually, it is of paramount importance to keep ourselves clear of the energies we are removing. If we don't, we can inadvertently take those energies on and get contaminated, congested, depleted, and ill ourselves.

Of course, you can absorb other people's energy even if you're not doing session work. It's more obvious in session work, so in a sense it's easier to remember to clear it, but it also happens in daily life when, for example, you talk to someone who's upset and releasing emotional energy and you start to feel upset yourself. If we're not being present in our bodies and aware of the dumping that's happening, we might forget that it's not our energy to process.

So whether you're in session or not, in the same physical space or not, using manual techniques or not, it's important to be aware of energy hygiene. Clearing your energy body daily is a self care practice just as essential as brushing your teeth.

Poor energetic hygiene is the number one cause of burn-out for those in the helping professions. I have a client who works as a massage therapist. In one of our sessions she mentioned her shoulder was hurting and she no longer had full range of motion with that arm. When I got into clearing the energy, I saw what looked like a mountain of energetic crud from her clients, which had lodged in her armpit. Once I cleared it she regained full range of movement again and was no longer in pain. With the awareness · that the pain and stiffness she was feeling was accumulated energy that her clients had released during session, she was able to be more conscientious about those energies at work and it was no longer an issue going forward.

We all have energy bodies, but most of us are not taught how to care for them. That's why this information on energetic hygiene is essential.

## ENERGY HYGIENE

Good energetic hygiene is so fundamental that I teach it on a regular basis as a stand-alone workshop for anyone who is interested. These techniques are game-changers and will help you to help more people and yourself simultaneously.

The most important thing you can do to keep sticky energies out of your field is to work from a "non-stick" state of mind. I call it compassionate non-attachment and it is an essential quality to cultivate, not only for healing work, but for healing your life.

Compassionate non-attachment means remembering that everyone is totally perfect already. Yes. Totally. Perfect. Already. This can be incredibly challenging when you find yourself looking at insanity and disease, but remember, the way things work in the invisible realms of consciousness are different than what we've been taught about the world through our social conditioning.

Maybe this perfection exists on a level that we can't possibly understand. Maybe because of that, it feels impossible to hold the idea of it in our minds. That may very well be, but we can still be open to the possibility that it exists. By being open to the possibility of perfection, you can free yourself from the sticky and limiting energy of judgment.

If you're really not feeling the perfection of the universe, you can simply say, "I don't know." Admitting that you don't know why situations or people are crazy is enough to take you out of judgment and attachment.

As you recall from the previous chapter on cord cutting, attachments are our beliefs, opinions, and preferences. What we think is right or wrong, good or bad. They're the stories we tell and the meaning that we've made out of everything we've experienced. In other words, they're all based entirely on the past.

If you'd like to create some new future possibilities, how helpful do you think it is to be operating under assumptions, conclusions, and decisions based on what occurred in the past?

You also learned in the last chapter that you can't clear something that you judge as wrong. If you are judging symptoms as wrong, they will stick to you. If you judge an energy as wrong, you can't clear it. If you have an attachment to fixing something you've judged as wrong, you can't be free of it. You can only be free by releasing attachment.

Simply put, focus on what you'd like to experience and release the attachment to it. It doesn't get any clearer than that. It may feel tremendously challenging at times to practice it, but isn't that what practice is for? Let's keep practicing compassionate non-attachment and set ourselves free from the prisons of recreating the past.

Focusing on what you'd like to create does not mean pretending like you feel fine when you are upset. It doesn't mean saying it's all love and light and ignoring the pain of the world. Remember, we have to feel it to heal it. We can't do a spiritual bypass of our trauma. We can't ignore our past.

What is truly healing is being the energy of unconditional love, recognizing we are upset and loving ourselves anyway. We can recognize that humans are a mess and love humanity anyway. We can recognize all the ways we hurt ourselves and each other and strive to do better. The way forward is with consciousness, acknowledgement, and love.

## ENERGY HYGIENE IN SESSION WORK

Now that we have identified what I have found to be the most helpful aspect of good energetic hygiene, the mindset of compassionate non-attachment, let's look at some more important things we can practice to keep ourselves clear as we're working.

• **Unity consciousness**: We know that we as our separate-selves are not doing the work, therefore we allow spirit to work through us and we know that love is the healer.
• **Sweep/flick energy**: We can manually sweep energy off of our hands/arms and flick it into a safe disposal place.
• **Disposal**: We can use a salt water bowl/psychic fire/center of the Earth/sun/source as a safe place to dispose of or compost congested/toxic energies.
• **Smudge/spray**: We can use a physical or psychic smudge or spray to purify our fields or hands as we work.
• **Cut cords**: We can release attachment to the outcome and to the client/session.
• **Gratitude**: We give thanks for being free of all toxic energies or attachments.

Some of these, like cord cutting, we've already covered. The new ones, like smudge and disposal, will be described below. If you practice energetic hygiene awareness with diligence, you will be able to work with greater capacity and longevity. Most importantly, you will be in service to yourself and that benefits everyone.

## SMUDGE SPRAY

I enjoy and recommend working with a liquid smudge spray. It's great when you are in a place where burning things is inconvenient or not allowed. No need to have lighters and bowls for ash, and it's much faster than burning smudge.

You can buy all sorts of smudge spray products, but I prefer to make my own because I run through a lot of it and it's more cost-effective. My stand-by is the simple formula I was introduced to through Pranic Healing. I've tweaked it over the years by adding crystal and flower essences, but you can start with the basic formula, which will serve you well.

The ingredients of an effective smudge spray are inexpensive and easy to find. The spray recipe is just a base of vodka with several drops each of tea tree and lavender essential oils. Tea tree oil contains abundant green energy, which is naturally cleansing and dissolving. The lavender oil has a lot of violet energy, which is cleansing and amplifying. When green and violet energies are used together, the effects are very cleansing.

To make the spray, get a clean glass spray bottle of two or four ounces, depending on the size you like to hold in your hand. Fill the bottle almost to the top with vodka, then add several drops each of the tea tree and lavender essential oils. Bless it up with a prayer, shake well, and you're good to go.

If you don't like having vodka around, you can also use rubbing alcohol diluted with water. I recommend using alcohol rather than just water because it is far more cleansing, both physically and psychically, and it dilutes the oils more effectively than water.

If you don't have a physical smudge, you can imagine a psychic clearing tool, like your hands or body in a green and violet flame that is burning away any energetic residue.

## SALT WATER BOWL

A bowl of salt water is an excellent tool to have on hand to collect any congested energy that you are clearing. As you are sweeping energy out with your light hands, you can flick it into the salt water bowl so that it's not just sitting around the room or landing in your field.

The water will naturally absorb energy and the salt will dissolve it. The salt to be used for cleansing is sodium chloride, aka sea salt or land salt. Sodium chloride crystals contain green energy, which has the natural qualities of cleansing and dissolving.

I like using salt water bowls because their physical presence reminds me to clear my field and my body as I work. I also program my bowl to absorb any energy my client releases in session. I do this simply by instructing the salt bowl, "Absorb any energy released in session today," or invoking, "It is my intent that the salt water absorb any energies released in session today."

If you don't have the physical tool, you can use a psychic tool. You can imagine a salt water bowl or a fire that you can throw things into. After using them, destroy them by disintegrating or extinguishing. My favorite psychic disposal tool is to shoot energies down into the fiery center of the Earth or up into the sun.

Psychic tools are awesome, they just require that you remember to use them.

## SWEEPING + FLICKING ENERGY

When clearing energies manually, it is essential to also clear them from your hands as you work. One way to do this is by spraying them with liquid smudge spray. Another technique is sweeping and flicking. Sweeping and flicking is a manual technique done with light body hands and fingers. Sweeping gathers the energy and flicking releases it. Using your long light body fingers of light, you sweep the energy off of your arms and hands, then you flick your fingers toward a safe disposal place, like a salt water bowl, and the energy flies off your hands and into the bowl.

When I'm in session I also smudge and sweep my head frequently because I am working a lot on the mental level and my head tends to get congested. I recommend sweeping or otherwise clearing any area of your field or body as soon as you notice any congestion.

Of course, if you are in a situation where you don't have a physical tool with which to work or you don't want to do manual clearing, you can always clear your field and hands with invocation or with imaginary tools like a psychic fire. The important thing is to maintain good hygiene throughout the session.

Now that we understand a bit more about how to safely keep our bodies and fields free of the energies we're clearing, let's get back to the details on sweeping and how to clear the biofield.

## CLEARING THE AURA OR BIOFIELD

Besides this new tool of manual sweeping, we already have a technique in our lightworker tool kit for clearing the biofield. Yep, it's our ol' pal invocation.

We can use invocation for anything and it is a fantastic technique to remember any time you are feeling stuck or aren't sure what to do. I use it all the time and I like to mix it up with various manual techniques as I go. I enjoy using a combination of mental and manual techniques because it feels balanced to me and I get information from both. As you practice, you may have periods of preferring some techniques above others, or circumstances when one technique may seem more appropriate than another. Go with the flow and trust that it's all good.

The auric biofield is actually multi-layered fields of various densities which can be cleared separately, but to start, let's go with an intention of clearing all the layers at once by focusing on the overall auric biofield.

## EXERCISE :: CLEAR THE BIOFIELD

When performing this clearing, you can practice on yourself remotely in a similar way to how you practiced cutting cords on your own back. You can intend or imagine that you are standing before yourself. You can also practice on a willing volunteer. Remember to always get permission for every session.

Here are the steps for clearing the auric biofield manually:

**1.** Invoke.
**2.** Set your intention to clear the auric biofield of the person with whom you're working.
**3.** Have this person stand in front of you, or imagine them in front of you.
**4.** Imagine your light fingers extending out two or three feet from your physical hands.
**5.** Position your hands with palms facing down, fingers together and extended, pointing toward the person whose field you're clearing. Extending the fingers strengthens those long beams of light coming out of them. These long beams of light are what is doing the work.
**6.** Starting with hands together at the center line at the top of the biofield, begin to sweep your long, beaming hands of bright light down the center line to the bottom of the biofield, following the curve of the spherical field.
**7.** At the bottom, scoop and flick the congested energy collected by your light hands into a safe disposal place like salt water or fiery center.
**8.** Then bring the hands to the top of the biofield again, this time with the hands spaced out about a foot from each other, and sweep down to the bottom, following the curve of the field. At the bottom, scoop and flick into disposal place.
**9.** Return to the top again, this time spacing the hands out about two feet, sweep down following the curve, scoop and flick.
**10.** Return to the top and space hands about three or four feet, imagining you are getting all the way out to the side of the biofield, sweep down, scoop and flick.
**11.** After performing this "one round" of sweeping on the front of the biofield, sweep the energy off your arms and hands into a safe disposal place and clean your hands with smudge spray or intent.

**12.** Repeat steps three through nine on the back side of the biofield.

**13.** Repeat another round of clearing on the front and the back of the biofield. Do about three to four rounds total or repeat until the energy feels clear.

**14.** When you feel complete, give thanks and clear your space.

When working with the body's biofield, it is helpful to remember it is not just a bubble of energy, but an energy dynamic that surrounds and interpenetrates the body. So as you are clearing it, imagine or intend that those very long beams of light coming off your fingers are penetrating all the way to the center of the field.

As you are sweeping through the biofield, you may sense the presence of congested energy, especially down the center line where the major chakra fields intersect the central channel of the field. As you sweep energy out, you may feel sensations in your hands, get pictures in your mind, or see energies clairvoyantly. You may also appear to get no feedback at all. Whatever you sense or don't sense is okay. The important thing is your intention. The energy will follow your intention whether you perceive something or not.

When I first started doing lightwork, my mind was very chatty and I was filled with doubt in my ability, so to keep a clear intention I would repeat it like a mantra in my mind, over and over, "I am clearing the field, I am clearing the field." It gave my over-active mind something to do, which was helpful. I was also not very adept at sustaining visual imagery, so I would use the "mantra" then, too.

If you have a wandering mind, a mind that talks back, a mind that seems to only run on overdrive like mine did, see if you can creatively channel some of that mind power into something helpful. All of our sensitivities and idiosyncrasies are unique talents and super powers just waiting to be used for the forces of light, love, and liberation.

Now that we have explored clearing the overall biofield surrounding and interpenetrating the body, there is another aspect of the larger light body with which you may choose to work. That aspect is the rays of light we emanate.

## THE RAYS OF LIGHT YOU ARE

Did you know you are a shining star? And within the star you are, there are more stars? Just like the toroidal fields within fields, we are a center of light that contains other centers of light and these centers radiate beams of light called rays. You have rays of light that emanate from star-like energy centers within you and radiate out through your field in all directions. The most powerful stars in your light body are in the center of your field, just below the heart, and at the top, just above the crown.

Sometimes these rays of light can get blocked or feel depleted. In truth, our light can never be diminished, but it can appear that way due to the power that our mind has to project its thoughts. If the mind is projecting thoughts of darkness, it can look as though a part of the body or field is shrouded in darkness and it will feel dark, but the rays are still there, shining unseen.

Similar to the fields, which are naturally balanced, we can seem to upset the balance and deplete the light of our rays through our unhelpful thought systems and beliefs. It is astounding how much our thoughts affect our experience and it is a true testament to the power of the mind. Isn't it wonderful that we can choose to use our mind power intentionally to create more beauty, harmony, and peace instead?

Knowing about the rays and that they can sometimes feel less than radiantly glorious, we can work with their energy to remind ourselves of our inherently shiny nature. You can use a mental technique like invocation to clear the rays. You could use a visualization to clear the rays, like imagining that you have a point of light at every major chakra center that is radiating out beams of light. You can also use the manual technique described below.

The rays of light surrounding us can be cleared, strengthened, and encouraged to stretch out by a manual technique of "combing" them with our light fingers. Similar to sweeping the biofield with our long hands of light, we can use our light hands with outspread fingers to comb through the rays. For clearing the biofield we worked along a spherical shape, but for the rays, we will be working from the center outward and combing out in all directions.

## EXERCISE :: CLEAR THE RAYS

Like all the other lightwork techniques, you can choose to work on yourself or a willing volunteer.

Here is the manual technique for clearing the rays:

**1.** Invoke.
**2.** Set your intention to clear the rays of the person with whom you're working.
**3.** Place or imagine that person in front of you.
**4.** Imagine your long, bright fingers of light extending out a couple feet from your physical hands.
**5.** Position your hands with palms facing out, backs of hands facing each other, fingers stretching out and spread like rakes. Extending the fingers strengthens those long beams of light coming out of them.
**6.** Starting with the backs of your hands together at the center of the light-body with which you are working, begin to comb the rays of light from the center outward with your long fingers of bright light.
**7.** At the outer edge of the rays, scoop and flick the congested energy collected by the fingers of light into a safe disposal place (eg: salt water or fiery center.)
**8.** Bring your hands to the center again, this time holding the hands at a different angle, comb the rays from the center out to the edge, scoop and flick into a disposal place.
**9.** After a couple rounds of combing, clear your hands with smudge spray or intention and sweep the energy off your arms and hands into a safe disposal place.
**10.** Continue to comb from center outward with your long fingers of bright light, changing the hand placement until all parts of the rays have been combed out.
**11.** Be sure to flick/sweep/smudge the energy off your hands as you work, always disposing of it in a safe place.
**12.** When you feel complete, give thanks and clear your space.

As you work, it is helpful to add your imagination/intention of the rays shining out strong and healthy. You may notice some places feel more congested. It may feel like the rays are all tangled up in a knot. You may wish to give these areas a little more TLC and gently comb them out.

## THINGS TO KEEP IN MIND

Often, when clearing the biofield, you will start to notice energy patterns or notice where there tends to be more congestion in the body. For example, maybe you are sensing a lot of congestion around the head and left hip. It can be helpful to make a mental note of this. That way, if you decide to clear on a deeper level, you'll know which areas to check. We'll be looking at this more in the next chapter on clearing specific chakras.

Another thing that can come up in clearing the field is having an awareness that cords have returned and require further extraction. If you have trouble getting all the roots out, use an invocation to do it.

At any time during a clearing, you may be aware that there are some known or unknown energies or entities in someone's space. No need to fear. You can use invocation to clear them, too. Simply intend that all unhelpful energies and entities be cleared and that anything that doesn't allow that also be cleared.

Remember, if you ever feel stuck in a process, or if you pick up on some kind of energy that you're not sure how to clear, use your invocation technique. You are never doing this work alone.

## CHAPTER 7 :: KEY POINTS

- There are abundant, free, and easy tools for clearing energy all around you.
- There are many levels of the energy body with which we can work.
- The overall biofield and the chakra fields of the body are toroidal fields.
- Toroidal fields are a self-sustaining energy dynamic.
- We can clear our biofields and rays of light mentally or manually.
- While clearing, it is important to maintain energetic hygiene.

- The key to energy hygiene is non-attachment or non-judgment.
- The key to clearing energy is also non-attachment or non-judgment.

## CHAPTER 7 :: INTEGRATION TIPS

- If you find yourself having judgments, delete them by cutting cords or invoking.
- If you find that you picked up some funky energy throughout the day, use the invocation to clear it as soon as you are aware of it.
- Invoke to cut cords and clear your biofield every night before bed.
- In the morning, use a smudge spray to clear your bed before making it.
- Make a travel smudge spray to carry with you and use throughout the day.

## CHAPTER 7 :: PRACTICUM POSSIBILITIES

**Practicing Forgiveness:** (5 to 10 minutes)

In the section on energy hygiene, we emphasized the importance of compassionate non-attachment for keeping ourselves clear of sticky energies. This cultivation of non-judgment is not only helpful in lightwork sessions, but also an essential practice for freeing ourselves of all painful judgments that cause our suffering. True forgiveness is non-judgment. True forgiveness will set us free from the mental patterns that drain our energy and weigh us down with emotional baggage.

Practicing forgiveness every day is highly recommended to master your own egoic mental patterns. Try these intentions as a template and then feel free to explore language or visuals that feel most potent for you:

- "I am thankful to be partnering up with the infinite mind of creation to release any and all judgments, opinions, stories, and the meanings that I've made so that I may be clear to receive the knowingness of the perfection that already is. I let it be, and so it is."
- "Spirit, I am willing to release all my ideas about this to you. Thank you

for clearing all unloving thoughts and judgments from my mind forever."
• "I am only interested in seeing all through eyes of love."
• "Universe, I don't know what anything means, but you do. Show me."
• "I am so grateful to release anything that blocks my perception of truth now."

**Noticing Energy Patterns:** (10 - 15 minutes)

As you are working to clear energetic congestion in the biofield, you may start to pick up some information. For this exercise, practice clearing the field of yourself or a volunteer and pay attention to the following:

• Do you notice more congestion in certain parts of the body or biofield? Where is it?
• Get curious. Ask a question like, "What does this energy feel like?" "What does it look like?" "Does it have a color or shape?" "Does it have temperature or texture?"
• Notice any information you might receive.
• Notice if some areas in the biofield or body seem to have more energy or less energy.
• Get curious about the balance of energy in the field. Does it feel balanced side to side, front to back, top to bottom?
• What are some things that pop into your mind as you work? Is there other information you are picking up on?
When you finish clearing the field, notice if you feel like something is incomplete or unfinished. If so, invoke for completion.

Take a moment to reflect on your findings with an open mind. Resist the temptation to draw conclusions and allow it to just be interesting information.

If you worked with a friend, ask what they felt. Share your experiences with each other.

**Dive deep**

you are that

well of mystery
reflecting yourself

eternal expression of
evolving consciousness

gazing into the pool
at the core of its being

center of centers
observer observed

you are the fingertip
breaking the surface

you are the infinite
depth of each droplet

you are the stillness
of spiraling movement

and the twining polarities
of opposites uniting

# CHAPTER 8:
# CHAKRA FORM +
# FUNCTION + CLEARING

*I am the mystery and so am I*

## FIELDS WITHIN FIELDS

As we learned in **Chapter 7: Energy Clearing + The Biofield**, every body has a corresponding field of energy that surrounds and interpenetrates it. One of the cool things about the holographic nature of the universe is that if you understand one part of it, you understand all parts of it. So, if you know how a larger energy field operates, you can extrapolate that to the smaller fields within it.

The electromagnetic biofield of the human body is a microcosm that contains unknown quantities of fields within it. For example, within the biofield of the body, you have the chakral fields that govern systems of the body. Within the chakra fields there are the smaller fields of individual organs. Within that, the even smaller fields of the cellular bodies that make up the tissues, and within the cells, the tiny fields of subatomic particles. The smaller bodies and fields are nested inside the larger ones, like a fractal version of Russian nesting dolls.

The human body is also a smaller body within a larger organism, so the biofield of the human body is a smaller field within the vastly larger field of the human collective. That collective field is contained within the larger field of the Earth, which is in turn contained within the even larger field of the solar system, which is within the field of the galaxy, which is within the field of the universe.

All of these energy fields are toroidal. A toroidal field is balanced by the movement of opposing forces. As we discovered, the fields are spiraling energy in opposing directions. For the overall biofield of the body, that energy is moving up and down. On the chakra level, the fields are perpendicular to the central channel of the body's field, so the energy is spiraling front to back.

All fields are centers of consciousness. Chakras are centers of consciousness. They are so much a part of us that we take them for granted. Like the stomach, for example. You may not understand exactly how it functions, but you can still work with it.

Like all centers of consciousness, chakras have a kind of intelligence. And like all centers of consciousness, the chakral fields are evolving.

## EVOLUTION OF THE HUMAN ENERGY FIELD

When I started learning lightwork techniques, I trained in and practiced the chakra-based energy work system of Pranic Healing that had precise protocols for specific conditions. So, after five years of daily practice, I was very adept at accurate energy scanning to get clear information about the state of people's energy fields.

In late 2012, I started to get a sense that there was something developing in the energy fields of clients that I hadn't seen before. I first noticed it when I was clearing the universal channel of energy above a client's crown. It felt like I was clearing the central channel of the body, because I could feel bumps of energy. In the central channel of the body, those bumps are the energy fields of the intersecting chakras. But in the universal channel, there weren't any chakras above the crown, were there? Not according to the

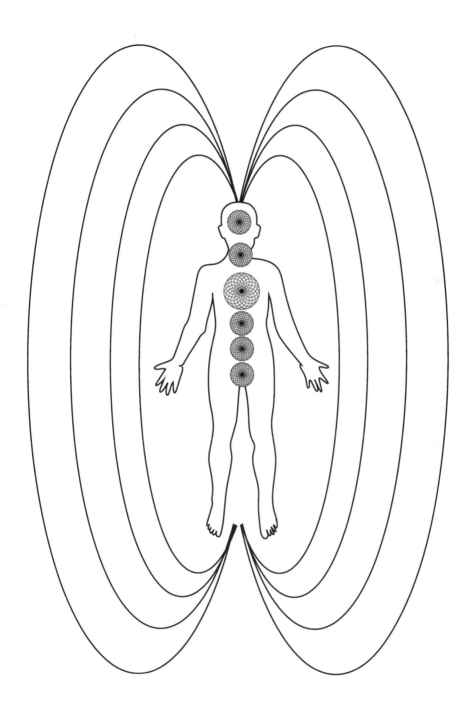

*Major chakras of the human body*

teachings I had received.

The entity incident mentioned in **Chapter 6** had already happened, so rather than spend any time doubting myself, I went straight to more inquiry and scanning. I asked, "Are these chakras?" The answer was, "Yes." I was excited. I had never seen this before. When I used specific scans to investigate, I found that there were two more chakras opening above the crown, and there were a couple more beyond that which hadn't started to open yet.

After the session, I scanned myself. Sure enough, I was developing extra crown chakras, too. I asked if there were others developing like this and got a "yes." I kept inquiring and doing session work and I found that different people were in different stages of development, but everyone I scanned was developing to some degree. I also found that the more open and loving people were, the faster the chakras developed. Fear seemed to shut down or slow the process.

After a couple months it was clear to me human energy fields were evolving to have at least five more chakras above the crown and at least three more below the root. I started calling the ones above the crown spiritual chakras and the ones below the root Earth chakras.

As time went on, I discovered more about them and the mysterious process of evolution that was unfolding. It turns out that there are existing stories of advanced yogis or spiritual masters developing these extra chakras, but what I witnessed was lay people developing their energy bodies in ways that previously could only be developed by initiates of specific esoteric training in isolated spiritual communities.

I would occasionally check in on the collective of humanity to see if everyone else, besides people I was working with, was also developing these extended chakra systems. I saw that though the folks who were drawn to work with me were often more on the leading edge of development, even people in the mainstream who didn't have a conscious spiritual practice were slowly ascending as well.

Within about three years, or around 2016, the evolution of the human energy field had reached a point at which everyone with whom I worked had successfully opened at least five chakras above the crown and three chakras below the root.

By the summer of 2017, we reached a tipping point. Enough humans had developed enough of the extra chakras in the central channel that there came a huge expansion of the body's biofield. I had seen a lot of amazing things in my work at that point, but it blew my mind when I saw clients' biofields expanding ten, twenty, some even thirty times larger than they had been before. The first time I saw it, I knew better than to doubt it. I just kept scanning, asking questions, being curious about the process, and asking how I could help.

This human energy field expansion happened fairly quickly. People's fields went through a massive expansion process during July and August of 2017. During the fall, the fields started finding some balance and equilibrium. By the time the winter came, the energy of the expansion started integrating into people's experiences. From around August 2017 to Spring 2018, many people were going through detox symptoms in their bodies, and shake-ups in their relationships, jobs, and mental health.

Similar to the expansion of chakras on the central channel, not everyone's field developed the same way. Some people who were really clear, like advanced lightworkers, had fields expand forty, fifty, even sixty times bigger. Even folks in the mainstream who weren't interested in consciously doing spiritual work expanded their fields, but only a few times times bigger, which frankly is still a huge energy shift for an unsuspecting citizen to process.

At the time of this writing in mid-2018, I am seeing that people are now developing even more chakras in the central channel, more spiritual and Earth chakras. It feels like we have reached the point at which energy flows easier and evolution unfolds more quickly. It's an exciting time to be witnessing and participating in this process.

I share this to emphasize that everything changes. Our energy bodies are evolving. Even things that don't appear to be evolving are evolving. We are surfing a wave of evolution. What's happening is a mystery. At the same time, we share one mind. Us, the wave, and all of nature are one consciousness, so in a sense we are the authors of this mysterious adventure we are experiencing.

I invite you to embrace the mystery. Dive in and explore. Enjoy the view on the leading edge of the tidal wave of evolution and don't worry about memorizing everything in this chapter on chakras. You will learn much through your practice and you can always refer to this text should you feel called. There's no shame in an explorer of energy consulting their notes.

Whenever I teach classes on chakras, it can get a bit intellectual, so I'm reminding all of us to be open to other ways of receiving information, like what you intuit about a chakra, how it feels, or what it looks like clairvoyantly. The chakra may even tell you something about itself. Everything has consciousness.

## CHAKRA FORMS + LOCATIONS

There are a few categories that I like to group chakras into for the sake of organizing the information. They are:

• Major chakras aligned on the vertical axis: crown, root, extended chakras.
• Major chakras on the horizontal axis: heart, solar plexus, head, etc.
• Minor chakras in other places in the body: spleen, hips, armpits, etc.

On the vertical axis of the central channel are the major chakras we call the crown and root. These chakras at the top and bottom of the central channel of the body are actually the upper and lower vortices of the body's biofield. They are the top and bottom of one field and run energy up and down. Because this field has many layers, you will find multiple vortices—or chakras—above the crown and below the root. I call the ones above the crown spiritual chakras and the ones below the root Earth chakras.

On the horizontal axis are most of the major chakras that most people are familiar with, like the solar plexus or heart. They intersect the central channel at a perpendicular angle and run energy front to back. These major chakras are fields within the biofield that source energy for specific systems, areas, organs, and functions of the body.

All throughout the body you will find a plethora of minor chakras for things like organs, joints, or even cells. Each part of the body has an energy field supporting it and these fields can be found on the smallest and largest bodies that we know of. Some important minor chakras include the hips, shoulders, spleen, hands, and feet.

Because we are in the midst of a great evolutionary shift in the human energy field, new chakras are developing quite rapidly. It is important to take all information from the past as a guideline and not a rule. This book contains the latest developments I am aware of at this time.

The following section is a breakdown of the energetic qualities and functions of the major chakras we will be working with in lightwork sessions. You may find it helpful to have a copy of the Chakra Chart given in the **Appendix** on hand for reference or note-taking as you go through.

In the naming of chakras, I follow the tradition of calling the top and bottom vortices of the larger field layers by different names, like the crown and root. I also follow the tradition of calling the other major chakras by one name subdivided front and back, for example: front solar plexus and back solar plexus.

Be aware that different schools of thought will organize the body's energy systems differently. None of them are right or wrong. All division is a convenient construct to assist us organizing our time and work. In reality, the body, like everything else, is one.

When working with this system or any other, pick what works for you and remember it's not ultimate reality, just a convenient way to work in manageable chunks. In other words, the system is in service to you, not you to it.

## LOCATIONS + FUNCTIONS OF MAJOR ENERGY FIELDS OF THE BODY

### VERTICALLY-ALIGNED MAJOR CHAKRAS:

### EARTH CHAKRAS:

• Lower vortices of body's biofield, located below feet, opposite the spiritual chakras.
• Connection to Earth/embodiment, essential for health of physical body.
• Bring Earth energy up and ground spiritual energy down.
• Carry ancestral energy, energy of the physical body's bloodline.
• Currently expanding as the human energy field evolves.
• Strong, clear Earth chakras are essential for grounding.

### ROOT CHAKRA:

• Lower vortex of body's biofield, located at the perineum, opposite the crown.
• Connection to Earth/embodiment.
• Associated with physical body, survival, and ancestors.
• Brings Earth energy up, grounds spiritual energy down.
• Negatively affected by anxiety and trauma.
• Typically a bit smaller than other chakras.
• Tends to be much smaller than crown, but easily balances it at about a quarter of the size.
• Healthy root is essential for grounding and balancing spiritual/crown energy.

### CROWN CHAKRA:

• Upper vortex of body's biofield, located at top of the head, opposite root.
• Draws universal energy down, accesses spiritual skills/universal intelli-

gence.

• Associated with pineal gland, brain, nervous system, claircognizance.
• Brain is a delicate organ sensitive to over-energizing (energize crown with care.)
• Negatively affected by depression.
• Typically larger than other major chakras.
• Open, clear crown is important for lightworkers to channel universal energy.

## SPIRITUAL CHAKRAS:

• Upper vortices of body's biofield, located above the head, opposite the Earth chakras.
• Connection to universal energy/information.
• Draw down universal energy, transmit Earth energy up.
• Carry soul and multidimensional energy, spiritual skills.
• Currently expanding as the human energy field evolves.
• Strong, clear spiritual chakras are important for accessing spiritual energy/information.

## HORIZONTALLY-ALIGNED MAJOR CHAKRAS:

## BASE CHAKRA:

• Front and back vortices located at the pubic and coccyx bones.
• Lower physical center, center of body survival/support.
• Uses earth energy for maintenance and health of physical body.
• Related to physical health, survival, money, sex, home, family, primary partnerships, anything related to Earthly existence, feeling safe and supported.
• Negatively affected by fear and trauma.
• Associated with glands of ovaries/testes, reproductive organs, hips and legs, and entire structure of the physical body in general.
• Important for grounding and maintaining overall health and strength of

the body.

- Strong, clear base is essential for grounding spiritual energy.


## NAVEL CHAKRA:

- Front and back vortices located at the navel and low back.
- Higher physical center, center of physical life force energy and primal instinct.
- Front navel stores energy, back navel distributes energy.
- Front navel can be intentionally energized and packed with life force energy.
- Associated with the adrenal glands, low back, digestion/bowels, kidneys, eliminatory system, and overall physical energy levels.
- Related to physical life force energy, instinctual knowing, feeling safe.
- Negatively affected by unresolved trauma and entities.
- Back navel is typically smaller and is a common entity attachment zone.
- Strong, clear navel is essential for feeling safe, grounded, and energized.


## SOLAR PLEXUS CHAKRA:

- Front and back vortices located at the diaphragm and middle back.
- Lower emotional center, center of personal power and will.
- Important for self-worth, emotional health, healthy boundaries.
- Negatively affected by stress.
- Associated with the pancreas gland, middle back, diaphragm, stomach, liver, and all internal organs in general.
- Strong, clear solar plexus is essential for standing in your power.


## HEART CHAKRA:

- Front and back vortices located at the heart and upper back.
- Higher emotional center, center of love and connection.
- Associated with the thymus gland, physical heart, lungs, shoulders, arms, upper back, clairsentience, compassion, feelings of connection and unity.

- Physical heart is sensitive to over-energizing, safest to energize heart chakra from back.
- Like the crown, it can be much larger than other chakras.
- Negatively affected by belief in separation.
- Important for healthy immune system, feeling joy, bliss, connection.
- Strong, clear heart chakra is essential for lightworkers to channel the healing power of love.

**THROAT CHAKRA:**

- Front and back vortices located at the throat and back of neck.
- Lower mental center, center of concrete thought.
- Associated with the thyroid gland, physical throat, mouth, jaw, neck, hearing and clairaudience, application of knowledge.
- Related to oral addiction and addiction in general.
- Affected negatively by worry, over-thinking.
- Important for executing and expressing ideas, having a strong sense of trust.
- Back side is typically smaller than front and is a common entity attachment site.
- Strong, clear throat is essential for trusting your ability to channel universal intelligence.

**HEAD CHAKRA:**

- Front and back vortices located at the brow and occipital bone.
- Higher mental center, center of abstract thought and higher will.
- Master chakra associated with the pituitary (master) gland, endocrine system, head, some brain functions, sinuses, eyes, sight and clairvoyance, gateway to all other major chakras.
- Important for mental health, endocrine health, and balancing all chakras.
- Negatively affected by apathy, stress.
- Back side is typically smaller than front and is a common entity attachment site.
- Strong, clear head is essential for mastering your mind and all lightwork

skills.

## IMPORTANT MINOR CHAKRAS:

## SPLEEN CHAKRA:

• Located at the spleen, left side of torso.
• "Prana chakra" important for drawing in life force energy.
• Spleen is a delicate organ that is easily over-energized (gently energize chakra, not organ.)

## FOOT CHAKRAS:

• Located in soles of feet.
• Very important for grounding energy down and drawing earth energy up, especially for lightworkers.

## HIP CHAKRAS:

• Located in the inside crease of the hip joint.
• Important for giving (right side) and receiving (left side) earth energy.
• Related to feeling joy of embodiment.

## HAND CHAKRAS:

• Located in the palms of the hands.
• Important for giving (right hand) and receiving (left hand) heart energy.
• Important for lightworkers to clear during and after sessions.

## SHOULDER CHAKRAS:

* Located inside the underarm.
* Important for giving (right side) and receiving (left side) heart energy.
* Important for lightworkers to keep clear.

Please note, some people are energetically ambidextrous, in that they tend to receive more on the right side and give more on the left side or are equally balanced on both sides, so it's helpful to scan if you're not sure.

Each organ and part of the body has its own field, even if it's not mentioned here. When employing lightwork techniques, you can work on many different layers of the body.

For example, if there is upset in the stomach, you can clear the following parts of the body system, working from a more general to more specific level as follows:

**Level 1**: the overall field of the body
**Level 2**: the solar plexus chakra (nearest major chakra)
**Level 3**: the stomach chakra (specific minor chakra)
**Level 4**: the tissues of the stomach organ

You could even look at clearing the base chakra, because it is important for the health of the body in general. You can look at whether you feel there is a connection, perhaps mental or emotional, to another part of the body. Perhaps there is a connection to the throat and the oral energy there. Who knows?

You can go as deep as you like in exploring, but if you start to feel overwhelmed, no need to worry. Remember, through invocation you can always call on a higher intelligence to handle it for you.

Because chakras are centers of consciousness that have their own intelligence, you can work with them co-creatively in a lightwork session. Just like you can invoke a higher intelligence to clear a chakra for you, you can ask a chakra to clear itself. It will most likely take longer than if you were to do it, but you can combine techniques to work faster. Something to bear in mind as we get into chakra clearing.

## WORKING WITH CHAKRAS

Now that we know a bit about the form, location, and function of these chakras, let's look at working with them in lightwork sessions.

Here are some typical chakra conditions you will encounter in session work:

- Clogged or congested with old energy that needs to be cleared.
- Depleted and requiring an energetic infusion.
- Leaky and drained of energy.
- Over-active or under-active.
- Unbalanced.

Throughout this course we will examine each of these states in turn. In this chapter, we will be working with the technique for clearing chakras that are congested or clogged with stagnant energy.

First, we will require a means of discerning whether or not any congested energy is there to clear. You may already have ways of sensing this. If you are clairvoyant, you may see what it is. If you are clairsentient, you may feel what it is. If you are clairaudient, you may hear what it is. And if you are claircognizant, you may know what it is. If you aren't yet skilled in these senses or even if you are and would like confirmation of your intuition, you can use the following scanning technique.

This technique was a game-changer for me because it can be used for anything. I highly recommend mastering it.

## SCANNING ON A SCALE OF HOW MUCH

This is an excellent technique to use any time you would like to know how much of a certain energy exists. You simply hold an intention to sense the energy you would like to scan and then use your hands to feel for how much is there. You can also scan in your mind by asking to be shown a mental picture or number. But for now, we'll focus on the manual technique.

For our scan to be as accurate as possible, we can set up a scale. Imagine a scale of zero to ten, with zero being none at all and ten being the maximum amount. We imagine that this scale is in front of us and about two feet in length so that we can easily reach both ends of it with our hands. The zero end of the scale is on the left side and the maximum end is on the right.

When we manually scan for how much, we will use our hands as both marker and sensor. We'll use the left hand to hold the zero point marker at the left side and the right hand will be sliding down the scale toward it, sensing or scanning how much energy is registering on the scale. The right hand will start out past the maximum end of the scale and travel toward the zero point. Wherever it stops is where the energy is.

This may sound pretty wild at first, but it is really just another remote technique. It's similar to scanning how big your light body is, but this time instead of asking how big, we are asking how much and imagining the energy on a scale in front of us.

Similar to how we scanned for cords, when we scan on a scale of how much we will allow the hand to stop wherever it stops. You may feel the energy as tingling, pressure, a feeling that something's there, temperature change, a sensation in another part of your body, or maybe nothing at all. Maybe the hand just stops on its own. Trust your scan.

For the following scanning practice, pick a chakra to scan for energetic congestion. Follow along with the process described below and take your time to feel into it.

## EXERCISE :: SCAN HOW MUCH

**1.** Invoke.

**2.** Set an intention to scan for congestion in the chosen chakra. In your mind you may say, "I am scanning the _____ chakra for energetic congestion."

**3.** Imagine or intend that your scale of zero to ten is in front of you.

**4.** Hold your left hand on the zero end, palm facing toward the right. (You can use the whole hand or just a couple fingers) This hand will stay still, holding the zero point.

**5.** Bring your right hand out just past the maximum end, palm facing the left (whole hand or fingers) This will be the active scanning hand.

**6.** In your mind ask, "How much congestion is in \_\_\_\_ chakra?"

**7.** Start sliding your active right hand down the imaginary scale toward the left hand, noticing where the right hand wants to stop.

**8.** Trust that wherever the hand stops is where the energy is.

**9.** Give thanks.

How much congestion did you find? Was there a lot? A little? None at all? Try another chakra or two for the sake of fun and scientific inquiry.

Like any new technique, it will take a little practice to feel really comfortable with your scanning ability. If you ever get discouraged or confused, practice clearing that energy with an invocation, take a break, and come back to the practice refreshed.

On a technical note, some folks find it helpful when using the scanning scale to offset the hands a little bit so they aren't totally aligned on the same plane. That way, they're feeling more of the energy of the scan and not picking up so much on the energy of the hand chakras. For that same reason, some find it easier to use just the index and middle fingers for scanning with thumbs holding the other fingers.

Try using offset hands, both full hands, and just fingers to see what works best for you.

## HOW TO CLEAR A CHAKRA

Now that we know a way to determine how much energetic congestion is in a chakra, we can look at how to clear the congestion.

Like clearing the larger biofield, when clearing a chakra it can be very helpful to understand the structure to work more efficiently. When we are working on the chakral level, we are reaching into the swirling vortex of the toroidal field and sweeping out or pulling out energetic congestion and clogged-up energy.

What can help us work efficiently is to remember each chakral vortex is actually two toroidal vortices overlapping. One is spinning clockwise and one is spinning counterclockwise. The vortex spinning clockwise is pulling energy in toward the center of the chakra and as it exits the vortex on the other side, it's spinning counterclockwise and releasing.

Imagine yourself looking into the front solar plexus chakra. You are looking at the overlapping vortices. You are seeing energy being pulled in to the chakra clockwise and swirling toward the center. Simultaneously, you are seeing energy coming up and out from the center counter-clockwise and releasing.

Every chakra is spinning both ways, pulling energy in and releasing it continuously. The clockwise vortex is drawing energy in. The counterclockwise vortex is releasing energy out. Therefore, if we would like to release energetic congestion from a chakra, it will be much faster and easier if we follow the natural flow of the energy releasing out, which is counterclockwise.

For the following practice of manually clearing a chakra, we will be using a technique similar to clearing the biofield. Just like the biofield clearing, we will be using our big hands of light, sweeping them through the chakra, safely disposing of the energy we clear, and maintaining impeccable energetic hygiene as we work.

The only difference is that for this clearing, instead of sweeping the hands top to bottom and tracing the spherical shape, we will move like the spiraling vortex, sweeping our light hands in a circular motion counterclockwise, going with the flow of how chakras naturally release energy.

It is helpful to have your energy hygiene tools of salt water, smudge spray, or whatever you have handy to keep yourself clear as you work. Remember, if you don't have physical tools you can also use invocation or psychic tools for energetic hygiene.

It is also helpful to work the front and back vortices of the chakra individually. For example, work the front side of the solar plexus chakra and then the back side.

## EXERCISE :: CLEAR A CHAKRA

**1.** Invoke.
**2.** Pick a chakra with which to work. Choose to work with one side at a time, scanning the front or back.
**3.** Determine if the (front or back) chakra needs clearing by scanning for how much energetic congestion is there. Use the scanning technique described in the previous exercise.
**4.** If the chakra is not congested (you get zero on the scale), move on to the next side or the next chakra. If it is congested (more than zero), follow the steps below to clear it.
**5.** Imagine that the chakra vortex to be cleared is in front of you, about a foot wide.
**6.** Conveniently locate a safe disposal place directly below where you are working (for example, a salt water bowl right under the chakra).
**7.** With your big hand of light (I use my right hand) reach into the chakra and sweep counterclockwise with an intention of removing the congestion.
**8.** Spiral the hand out and flick the congested energy off of the hand and into a safe disposal place (salt water, psychic fire, etc.)
**9.** After a few sweeps of the chakra, clear your arms and hands by sweeping and spraying.
**10.** Rescan the chakra to see how much congestion is left.
**11.** Continue with sweeping and scanning until the chakra is completely clear and the scan reads zero on the scale of how much.
**12.** Give thanks and clear your hands.

Whatever intention you are holding in your mind is the energy you will be picking up on. Energy follows intention, so if you are sweeping with the intention of clearing and you feel your hand hitting something, it is a chunk of energetic congestion to clear. When you scan with the intention of finding cords and the hand hits something, it is a cord. When you have an intention of clearing and the hand hits something, it's something to clear. If you have an intention of energizing and the hand stops, it's something that needs energy.

If you hold a specific intention and don't feel or scan anything, then that particular energy is not there. If you are confused about any energy you're sensing, go back to your intention to clarify. If you are still unsure, you can invoke for assistance.

During a chakra clearing, if you repeatedly sweep and scan the same amount of congestion as before and the energy doesn't seem to be clearing, check to see if a cord has reattached. If you scan and find a cord, cut it and then go back to scanning congestion and clearing the chakra. It will most likely clear.

If you do the above steps and the chakra still feels congested, I recommend clearing with the invocation. If you have an idea of what the stuck energy is, you can add that to your intention. If you're not sure, you can hold an intention of "I am grateful that whatever this energy is, it is clearing now, and anything that doesn't allow that is also clearing now."

There is an abundance of interesting things that could pop up during healing sessions, so remember your invocation tool. It's perfect for dealing with all the mysterious things that arise, whether you can name them or not.

## OTHER KINDS OF LOCALIZED CLEARINGS

If you've looked at the Lightwork Session Protocol outline given in the Appendix, you may have noticed that there are three kinds of localized clearing listed. One of those, chakra clearing, we just covered, so let's look at the other two: channels and tissues.

## CLEARING TISSUES OF THE BODY

We've already done some clearing of the physical body tissues. Can you think of what it might be?

It is the energetic hygiene tool of sweeping the hands and arms to keep them free of the energies we are clearing. In that action, we are clearing a specific part or tissue of the body.

Sweeping the tissues of the body is as simple as that. We intuitively follow the natural contours of the body part we are clearing and sweep our light hands through it, flicking the congestion into a safe disposal place. We can clear muscle tissue, organs, fluids, bones, glands, skin, or any other part of the body.

Let's practice clearing tissues of the body by focusing on an organ. The liver is an organ that tends to accumulate some energetic congestion due to all the work it does for the physical and emotional bodies. Follow the steps below to give your liver some love:

## EXERCISE :: CLEAR TISSUES OF THE BODY

**1.** Invoke.
**2.** Imagine or intend that your liver is right in front of you. Don't worry if you don't know what a liver looks like. Spirit knows. (Bonus points for trusting AND bonus points for looking up anatomy illustrations.)
**3.** Use the scale technique to scan how much energetic congestion is in the liver. If you got zero, scan another organ to find some congestion to clear. If you got more than zero, continue on to the next step.
**4.** Imagine your long fingers of light sweeping from the top of the organ to the bottom.
**5.** Flick the energy off the hands into a safe disposal place.
**6.** Imagine you are rotating the organ to sweep the sides and the back, the top and the bottom.
**7.** Sweep and flick the energy and sweep your hands as you work to keep them clear.

**8.** Keep sweeping until the organ feels clear or until a scan shows no congestion.

**9.** Give thanks and clear your hands.

Sweeping parts of the body is helpful for clearing pain, tension, and stress from tissues, helping them to relax and heal.

For lightworkers, it is crucial that we sweep all of our arms, shoulders, upper back, neck, and head thoroughly because we move so much energy through our crowns, hearts, arms, and hands. You can sweep your own back by imagining you are standing behind yourself, with your back conveniently right in front of you. Try it out now. Sweep your head, too. It feels amazing.

............................................

## CLEARING CHANNELS

We've mentioned the central channel of the body when describing the human energy field. We've also encountered it in our meditation where we imagine an Earth channel going down from the root chakra to the center of the earth and a universal channel going up from the crown chakra to the sun or home star.

The universal channel, core channel, and Earth channel are all part of the central channel that can be divided into three parts for convenience. Clearing the Earth channel facilitates grounding. Clearing the core channel facilitates chakra flow. Clearing the universal channel facilitates connection to higher consciousness.

To clear a section of the central channel, simply follow the steps below.

## EXERCISE :: CLEAR THE CENTRAL CHANNEL

**1.** Invoke.
**2.** Decide which section of the channel you'd like to work with first: either the top/universal channel above the crown, the center/core channel in the middle of the body, or the bottom/Earth channel below the root.
**3.** Imagine that section of the channel in front of you, at a convenient size, no bigger than a few feet in length.
**4.** Scan to see if there is energetic congestion in the section you're working with.
**5.** If there is congestion, sweep your light hands down through the channel, flicking the congested energy into a safe container, maintaining excellent energetic hygiene by clearing your hands as you work.
**6.** Sweep and scan until the section is clear.
**7.** Move on to the next section: scan and sweep until clear.
**8.** Keep working through the sections until you have cleared all three.
**9.** Give thanks and clear your space.

As you are clearing the central channel, you may notice that you hit some bumps that feel like congestion, especially where the major chakras intersect the channel of the biofield. It could be congestion, a chakra, or both. Remember, we have chakras intersecting the core channel of the body that you may feel as you sweep that part of the central channel. We also have chakras above the crown and below the feet that you may feel as you sweep the universal channel or the Earth channel. Often, it is enough to simply sweep through the channel to remove the congestion, whether it is in the overall biofield or the smaller chakral field, but you can also go to a specific chakra-clearing technique if that seems more appropriate.

If you are familiar with other kinds of channels like acupuncture meridians in the body, you can experiment with clearing them, too. Simply sweep along the channel, following the flow and contour, flicking the hands into a safe container, and practicing good energetic hygiene as you work.

Remember, all manual techniques can be performed mentally. See the **Scan + Invoke Technique** in the **Practicum Possibilities** section below for a guide on how to do everything we've covered so far with just the tools of scanning and invocation.

Enjoy exploring the mystery.

## CHAPTER 8 :: KEY POINTS

- We contain infinite fields of electromagnetic energy.
- Different schools divide up the chakras differently.
- Chakras are toroidal fields.
- Chakras have consciousness.
- Chakras are moving clockwise and counterclockwise at the same time.
- You can scan a chakra to see how much congestion is there to clear.
- To clear energy from a chakra manually, go with the counterclockwise flow.
- You can clear chakras with the invocation.
- The scanning scale can be used for measuring "how much" of anything.

## CHAPTER 8 :: INTEGRATION TIPS

- Invoke to clear all chakras before going to sleep.
- Practice scanning with the scale technique any time you'd like to know "how much."
- While taking a salt bath, instruct chakras to release any congestion into the bath.
- Throughout the day, check in with your roots and crowns. Are they clear?
- If you feel ungrounded or disconnected, invoke to clear the central channel.

## CHAPTER 8 :: PRACTICUM POSSIBILITIES

**Scanning Practice:** (15–20 minutes)

First, cut cords. Then, using the **Chakra Chart** in the **Appendix** as a guide, practice going through the body, chakra by chakra, scanning for congestion. Use a system to help you stay organized as you work, like starting at the bottom back, going up the back, down the front, and ending on the bottom front, just like when you were cutting cords. Pick one or two chakras that had the most congestion and practice clearing them using the manual sweeping method.

**Scan + Invoke Technique:** (10–15 minutes)

First, cut cords if you haven't already, then scan chakras and find one that has some congestion to clear. Then rather than clearing it manually, use the invocation to clear it. You may state an intention like, "It is my intent that any and all energetic congestion be cleared from this chakra now." Either scan as you invoke to feel the energy receding, or invoke and scan again.

If there is still some energy there that is not clearing you may use an intention like, "It is my intent that anything that doesn't allow this energy to clear also be cleared now." Then scan again. Practice scanning and using different words and intentions to see which ones feel most potent. Note that that may change as the circumstances change and as your practice evolves.

**Creative Clearing with a Chakra:** (10–15 minutes)

For this practice we will go a bit outside the box. Knowing that everything has consciousness, we can work with the consciousness of the chakra or the body itself to facilitate healing. First, cut cords and scan to find a congested chakra. Then, instruct the chakra to clear itself.

To do so, imagine the chakra in front of you, point your hand at it and say, "_____ chakra, you will empty all energetic congestion into the salt water/center of the Earth now. Thank you."

It may take a while for the chakra to empty itself, but you could get one chakra clearing itself while you work on another one, so that you can save time.
Start with one, then try instructing two at the same time. Once you have

mastered this, you can go straight to the front head chakra, which is the master chakra, and instruct it to clear itself and all the other chakras. Then, while the chakras are clearing themselves, you can go in, mentally or manually, and help them to clear faster.

## A ray of light


you are the descendant
of the great central sun

infinite light
your birthright

flows of energy
ever repleted

information
live-streaming

its teaching received
you learn how to share it

aligned by its guidance
you will fly true

traveling far
yet ever present

a sure radiance
glowing with wisdom

the polished jewels
of experience shining

a beacon of light
leading home to your self

# CHAPTER 9:
# ENERGIZING + SEALING +
# HARMONIZING

*Love is the healer and I am love*

## PRINCIPLES OF ENERGIZING

So far in this course, we have been focused on clearing unwanted energy out of our systems. We've cleared cords, cleared auras, cleared our minds, cleared our bodies, and cleared chakras. Now we will turn to adding energy into our systems, also known as energizing.

There are four important principles to keep in mind when energizing: be a clear conduit, source transpersonal energy, clear before energizing, and hold a clear intention.

Let's break them down one-by-one.

## BE A CLEAR CONDUIT

To source and use universal energy effectively, lightworkers must be a clear channel. That means we must keep our own physical and energetic bodies clear enough that our personal blocks aren't getting in the way of the energy flowing through us. Otherwise, we may find ourselves getting frustrated, depleted, or having to work a lot harder than necessary. We could even project our own baggage onto others.

Working on your own energetic baggage and blocks is essential. It is a tremendously helpful and necessary contribution to the whole of humanity. You don't have to have it all perfectly dialed in before you work with others, but you can't avoid your own shadow work and still be successful. Shadow work is lightwork.

Fortunately, we have the tools to become a clear conduit. We can invoke. We can clear our biofield, chakras, and channels. And we are going to learn how we can strengthen our crown and heart chakras and the central channel of the biofield. This is helpful, because the more clear the pathway, the more easily the light can flow through us.

## SOURCE TRANSPERSONAL ENERGY

Though it is important to clear our personal fields, bodies, and channels to be a clear conduit, when we project energy, we are not using our body's personal energy for healing. We are using transpersonal, universal energy.

Universal energy is yours, but it's not only yours. It's an infinite supply for everyone and everything. When you tap into it, you will receive the benefit of that energy. So, not only will you not be depleted, you'll actually receive more energy.

Anytime you feel depleted, it's a good idea to check your ego, cut cords, and invoke for assistance. Remember, it's not the separate self that is doing the work. It's the true self, which is not alone, but one with all of creation.

## CLEAR BEFORE ENERGIZING

Just like it makes sense to clean a physical wound before applying medicine and dressing it with a bandage, it makes sense to clear congested energy out before energizing and shielding. Otherwise, we would likely be energizing and activating the very things we would like to release.

There are, in fact, some advanced techniques in which you energize before you clear, but even in those cases, the initial energizing is used to break up energetic congestion before removing it, so you clear right afterward. If you know this principle, you can apply it to session aftercare for any modality that focuses on energizing, like Reiki. If you receive a Reiki session, it will be helpful to do energetic clearing or take a cleansing salt bath afterward to help ameliorate any detox symptoms your body might have in response to the session work.

Thorough clearing before energizing significantly reduces the chances of us or anybody we're working with having a healing crisis. *Healing crisis* is the term for a detox reaction in the body after a session in which the symptoms that one is attempting to relieve actually become markedly worse for a period of time before subsiding. Healing crisis is common for folks who receive certain modalities of healing that focus on adding energy into the system. People can also experience healing crisis after receiving a spontaneous downpouring of light, a spiritual initiation, or an energetic attunement.

Healing crisis or detox symptoms also frequently occur when there is an amplified amount of light/energy entering the collective field of humanity. We are living in such a time. The light pouring into the collective is stirring up all the unhealed aspects of our collective psyche and bringing it up for healing. This will be addressed more in **Chapter 11: Additional Explorations** in the section on ascension symptoms.

In my session work experience of clearing well before energizing, only about one out of 400 recipients have had any kind of healing crisis reaction. Those few folks had longstanding physical health issues and tended to hold onto a lot of heavy energy. Even in those cases, the symptoms of healing crisis were mild.

Results will typically depend on how well you clear. When I'm in session, I go back and check multiple times to make sure I get everything that is possible to clear for that session. It may sound like a lot of work, but it gets much faster the more you practice. We can always invoke for help with clearing quickly.

Another major benefit of clearing old energy out before energizing is that, in many cases, once an area is cleared, the system will naturally be able to source more energy and balance itself without any extra energy required. This makes your work much more efficient. Typically, after systems self-balance, just a bit of energizing will be all that is required.

## HOLD A CLEAR INTENTION

The flow of energy is our arrow. Intention is our aim.

Because energy flows along the path of our intention, it is crucial to hold clear focus in our minds. It's especially important while energizing to be conscious of what we are focusing on, because we are amplifying our thoughts with more energy than usual.

When we are projecting energy into a field or body, we must hold a space, vision, or intention of the perfect result. The more we focus on the healing having already happened, the more effective we will be.

As soon as we identify an area in need of healing, we release the idea of its brokenness and instead focus on the perfect state of health. That way we are putting our creative energy into what we would like to see instead of what we would not like to see.

This is true of all our thoughts all the time. We are always creating through our mindset and intention, whether conscious or not. That's why this course focuses attention on the importance of the power of our minds and why we keep coming back to the technique of invocation, because these tools allow us to choose a powerful state of mind and set a clear intention.

Now that we've looked at the principles of energizing, let's get into the practical applications—or indications—for energizing.

## INDICATIONS FOR ENERGIZING

There are five major applications for energizing in session work:

1. Resolve depletion.
2. Seal leaks.
3. Harmonize or balance
4. Disintegrate or dissolve.
5. Create a psychic structure.

Let's look at each of these more closely.

## ENERGETIC DEPLETION

Energetic depletion means that there is a less than optimal amount of energy in a particular area. Energetic depletion typically occurs due to one of two things: either a block in the flow of energy, or an energy drain.

Stagnant energetic congestion or blocks can create a lack of fresh energy in our systems simply by blocking the flow. If energy is unable to travel where needed in our bodies, it can cause an energetic depletion in the deprived areas.

Energetic parasites, thought forms, and etheric cords or attachments drain energy. If energy is being siphoned off by one or more of these things, it could result in energetic depletion in part of the body.

Whatever the reason for the depletion, simply clearing the congestion, block, or drain may be enough to allow the system to balance itself. If not, adding a bit of energy into the system is indicated.

## ENERGY LEAKS

Sometimes depletion is caused by energetic leaks, which are a cause of energy drain. Leaks look like holes in the energy field and may be caused by a lack of structural integrity due to unhealthy boundaries, parasites, entities, cords, or even beliefs. If energetic depletion is complicated by a leak, the leak must be sealed and the structure strengthened in order for the energy to hold. If you energize a depleted area and when you scan it again nothing seems to have changed, check for a leak.

If you discern a leak, you can add energy in to seal it, then continue to resolve the depletion.


## HARMONIZE + BALANCE

Harmonizing and balancing refers to adjusting the size of the fields or channels so that they are in harmonious proportion and alignment.

Once the depletion and leaks are attended to, the chakras, channels and fields tend to balance and harmonize themselves, but sometimes it is necessary to make an adjustment to the activity level of an area to bring the energy back into balance.

The activity level is determined by the size of the energy field or channel. Fields and channels can sometimes be overactive/too big, or under-active/ too small. Because healthy activity level depends on the field/channel, the day, the person, and many other factors, it is wise to scan to find the ideal size for that moment, compare to the actual size, and make any necessary adjustments.


## DISINTEGRATE OR DISSOLVE

Not only is energizing useful for constructing or repairing, it can also be used with the intention of disintegrating or dissolving something, like an energy block. Imagining your hands in a violet flame is a way of adding energy to dissolve. The technique for dissolving cords with light given in the practicum section of **Chapter 6** is another example.

## PSYCHIC STRUCTURES

Psychic structures are energetic forms we create for a specific purpose such as filtering, protecting, shielding, clearing, or sealing. Psychic fires, like the ones we worked with in **Chapter 7: Energy Hygene + Biofield Clearing**, are a kind of psychic structure created for the purposes of clearing or disposing of energies safely.

Other examples of psychic structures include energetic grids, seals, containers, wards, circles, bubbles, mock-ups, mirrors, funnels, generators, and shields.

The main psychic structures we will be working with in this text are shields. Shields are like an energetic bandage or filter that is put on at the end of a session to protect the work that has been done. In **Chapter 10: Shielding + Sealing the Process**, we will learn and practice a technique for shielding.

## HOW TO PROJECT ENERGY

Now that we have an idea of the reasons why we energize, let's explore some hows.

You already know that you can use invocation for anything, and energizing is no exception. So, if you ever feel stuck while practicing the following techniques of manual energy projection, you can invoke and have source consciousness do it for you.

When learning how to project energy effectively, it is crucial to practice techniques that will not drain your body's personal energy supply. Therefore, we will practice tapping into universal or transpersonal energy sources. We have already set ourselves up for this by beginning every session with an invocation, but when it is time to project energy it is helpful to remind ourselves of our connection and focus on receiving. Receiving is the key to sharing, after all.

We receive life force energy through our breath. We receive energy through all of our chakras and fields. We bring in energy through our Earth channel and universal channel, from nature, from our food and water, and of course, from the light of source energy/universal consciousness.

It is important to recognize that you and your hands are already hard-wired to receive and project energy. In fact, you have already done it. When a part of your body is hurt, you instinctively bring your hand to it. When you place your hand on something in this way, you automatically send some healing energy out of your hand to that part of your body. When someone is sad and you place your hand on their shoulder, you are sending healing energy to them.

When you learn to do this consciously with intention, your natural ability will become a powerful healing technique.

## EXERCISE :: PROJECT ENERGY

**1.** Invoke.
**2.** Sit with your back straight and relaxed, breathing deeply and gently.
**3.** Remember or re-imagine your Earth channel connecting you to the Earth and your universal channel connecting you to your home star.
**4.** Allow the tip of your tongue to touch the roof of your mouth.
**5.** Soften your face muscles or smile gently.
**6.** Raise your arms up a bit with hands open to the sky in a receiving gesture.
**7.** Feel gratitude for your connection to source energy.
**8.** Imagine that love light consciousness is flowing in from your crown and going down to your heart.
**9.** Keep your left palm up and open to continue receiving as you turn your right palm to face forward.
**10.** Feel or imagine a beam of white light coming out of the palm of the right hand, projecting out a few feet in front of you.
**11.** Breathe, relax, and notice the sensations in your body.
**12.** After a few rounds of breath, release the hands and the energy.

What did you notice? Could you feel a difference in the energy of your hands? What did it feel like? Perhaps you saw something or had an awareness of some kind.

After getting the feeling of projecting energy, try this:

**1.** Hold up the right hand, palm facing out.
**2.** Using the left hand, scan or feel the energy around and in front of the right hand.
**3.** Now, imagine you are projecting a beam of light out of your right hand.
**4.** Using the left hand again, scan the right hand and the area in front of it.

Was there a difference? Perhaps you are able to discern, through feeling or seeing, the difference between a hand that is not projecting energy and a hand that is. If you don't feel a difference just yet, that's okay. It is still happening.

In all the years I've been assisting my teachers and teaching my own classes, witnessing hundreds of students, I have seen that every single person has the ability to project energy. Like I said, we are hardwired to do this. If you get stuck or worried, use the invocation to clear your worries and invoke to do the thing you are feeling stuck on.

## PRACTICAL APPLICATION OF ENERGIZING

In practice, we don't typically energize unless it is indicated, so how can we tell if energizing is indicated or not? We can tell by using our scanning technique.

To scan for depletion, we use the same technique as we did for congestion— the scanning scale of how much—only this time, instead of an intention of scanning for how much congestion to clear, we scan with an intention of finding how much depletion to energize. If you are unclear on that technique, go back and review **Exercise :: Scan For How Much** in **Chapter 8: Chakra Form + Function + Clearing.**

In cases of depletion, before energizing it is important to clear your hands of all the energy you have been clearing, so be sure to spray them and sweep them thoroughly. That way you won't be inadvertently projecting any of that gunk back into the field.

If you recall, to make our clearing more effective, we swept the congestion out of the chakra in the direction the chakral vortex spins when it releases energy, namely, counterclockwise. In a similar fashion, if we'd like to make energizing more efficient, we can go with the flow of the chakral vortex as it draws energy in, which is clockwise. To do this, we imagine the chakra in front of us and project a beam of light into it, gently circling the projecting/right hand in a clockwise spiral.

Because energy follows intention, when we were clearing congestion we could sometimes feel our hand want to stop in an area where there was a chunk of congested energy. Similarly, when we are energizing a depleted area, if we feel the projecting hand want to stop, that is where the depletion is. You may even sense it as a hole, a dip, or a tear. We can use this awareness to put some extra attention in that area.

Whatever your intention is, that is what you will be picking up on. When you focus on clearing, your hand will feel what needs to be cleared. When you focus on energizing, your hand will feel what needs to be energized.

When you are energizing, the energy you project will also follow a specific intention of what you'd like that energy to do. You can project energy with the intention of sealing a leak, strengthening a depleted area, activating something to make it bigger, inhibiting something to make it smaller, or dissolving something completely. The white light we are projecting through our hands has the qualities of all colors and can perform any of those tasks, so it is our intention that gives shape and purpose to what the light is doing for us.

Make sense? Cool. Let's practice. We'll go through the steps we have so far and add in the new piece on energizing.

## EXERCISE :: ENERGIZE A DEPLETED CHAKRA

**1.** Invoke. (Technique given in **Chapter 5**)

**2.** Cut cords on the field and the chakras. (**Chapter 6**)

**3.** Clear congestion in the body's biofield. (**Chapter 7**)

**4.** Scan chakras for congestion and pick one that has the most to clear. (**Chapter 8**)

**5.** Clear the chosen chakra of energetic congestion until it scans as clear. (**Chapter 8**)

**6.** Clear your hands well of any of the energies you've been clearing. Sweep and use smudge spray or a psychic tool.

**7.** Scan the chosen chakra for depletion by using the scanning scale of "how much" and having a clear intention to scan for, "How much depletion is in this chakra?"

**8.** If the chakra has no depletion, go to another chakra and clear it before scanning for depletion. Do this until you find a depleted chakra.

**9.** Make sure your hands are free of energetic residue after clearing.

**10.** Imagine, or intend, that the depleted chakra is right in front of you.

**11.** Use the projecting technique: intend to connect with universal energy, left hand palm up and receiving, right hand palm forward and projecting.

**12.** Send a beam of white light into the chakra with the intention of energizing the depletion.

**13.** As you project, gently circle the right hand in a clockwise direction.

**14.** Remember to breathe and receive. (Feel gratitude and smile inside. It helps.)

**15.** If you sense where the depletion is, you may choose to make some tiny circles specifically in that area, otherwise just energize as usual.

**16.** After a few rounds of breath, and few circles around the chakra, pause and scan again for how much depletion.

**17.** Notice if the amount of depletion went down.

**18.** Continue to project energy and scan for depletion levels until the chakra is no longer depleted/you get to zero on the scanning scale.

**19.** Give thanks and clear your hands.

If you are adding energy into a chakra and the level of depletion doesn't seem to be going down when you scan it, chances are you've got a leak. You don't have to know why there is a leak or what is causing it, you can simply scan to find the presence of leaks and then energize with the intention of sealing them. As always, if you sense something that you're unsure of how to deal with, use the invocation and let spirt take care of it for you.


## EXERCISE :: SEAL ENERGY LEAK

Here's how to seal energetic leaks:

**1.** Using the scanning scale of "how much," scan, "How much energy is leaking from this chakra?"
**2.** If you scan how much and get a reading of zero energy leaking, use the invocation to clear, "Whatever is not allowing this chakra to hold energy." Then go back to energizing for depletion as shown in the previous exercise.
**3.** If you get a reading that there is indeed some energy leaking, follow the steps below to seal the leak.
**4.** To seal leaks, use the projecting energy technique: Imagine the chakra in front of you, intend to receive source energy (left palm upwards/right palm outwards), send a beam of white light out of the right hand, and circle the right hand clockwise as you intend to, "seal, strengthen, and repair this chakra."
**5.** If you feel your projecting hand want to stop, that's where the leak is, so you can add some more energy in that spot.
**6.** Imagine the light sealing the leaks and the chakra being strong.
**7.** Scan again to see if there is any leakiness left.
**8.** Keep projecting and scanning until all leaks are sealed.
**9.** Once the leaks are sealed, go back to energizing for depletion as described in the previous exercise.

Once you seal the leaks, the chakra should hold the energy and the depletion should rapidly abate as you energize. If you get that it is still depleted after sealing and energizing, use the invocation, "It is my intent to seal, strengthen, repair and energize this chakra in the perfect way, and anything that doesn't allow that is cleared through all dimensions and all bodies now."

Give thanks. You just did your first energizing and sealing practice. Now that you've learned the manual technique, let's look at an alternate way of energizing.

## EXERCISE :: RESOLVE DEPLETION WITH INVOCATION

As you've learned, any manual technique can also be performed with the tool of invocation. For this exercise, we will practice using a combination of scanning for how much depletion and invoking to energize it.

**1.** Scan to find a chakra with depletion.
**2.** Before resolving the depletion, first scan the chakra for congestion.
**3.** Using the manual or invocational technique, clear the chakra of congestion.
**4.** Scan again to make sure the congestion is clear.
**5.** If it feels like something is blocking the clearing, invoke to release it with: "It is my intent to clear whatever is not allowing this chakra to clear."
**6.** Keep scanning and invoking until the chakra is clear.
**7.** Clear your hands.
**8.** Next, scan the chakra for depletion.
**9.** If there is no depletion, repeat the above steps until you find a chakra that is depleted.
**10.** Using invocation, energize the chakra: "It is my intent that this chakra be energized in the perfect way."
**11.** Scan again.
**12.** If the depletion doesn't resolve, scan for leaks.
**13.** If there are leaks, use invocation to seal leaks: "It is my intent that any energy leaks be sealed in the perfect way."
**14.** Continue to scan and invoke until the depletion is resolved.
**15.** Give thanks and clear your hands.

## ENERGIZING TO HARMONIZE

As mentioned earlier, one of the five reasons we add energy to something is to adjust the size of it. When the biofield, chakras, and channels of the body are adjusted in this way they come into a harmonious balance.

The size of a chakra or channel is also called the activity level, because there is a correspondence. When a chakra or channel becomes more activated, it gets bigger. When it becomes less activated, it gets smaller. By inquiring and scanning, you can determine if something is balanced, underactive, or overactive.

Sometimes cutting cords, clearing congestion, resolving depletion and sealing leaks will be enough to allow a chakra to balance itself. In cases where it's not enough, it will be a great help to add some energy for the purpose of adjusting the activity level to one that is in harmonious balance with the rest of the system.

When energizing to harmonize, it is important to first scan the energy of a chakra to see what the current size is and if it requires an adjustment. To do this, we will learn and practice a new scanning technique.

Scanning for the activity level of a chakral field is a technique similar to one we encountered in **Chapter 6: Scanning Energies + Cord Cutting** when we learned to sense energy by scanning the etheric body or light body. In that exercise, we were feeling for the edge of that layer of energy around the physical body to see what size it was.

In the following scanning exercise, we will work remotely. We will imagine that the chakra we are scanning is right in front of us, and we'll use our hands to feel the edges of it as described below.

## EXERCISE :: SCAN CHAKRA ACTIVITY LEVEL

Work with a chakra from the previous practice of energizing, one that it is already cleared and ready to go.

**1.** Feeling connected, centered, and relaxed, imagine that chakra in front of you.
**2.** Raise your open arms, hands out on either side of the chakra, right and left, with palms facing each other.
**3.** Hold an intention in your mind of scanning to find the actual size of the chakra as it is now. "I am scanning the actual size of this chakra" or "Show

me the actual size."

**4.** Slowly bring your hands toward each other, pausing wherever you feel any sensation or the hands just stop on their own. That's the size or activity level of the chakra.

**5.** Now, to see if there is an adjustment required, scan again, only this time scan with the intention of finding the ideal size of the chakra. "I am scanning the ideal size of this chakra," or, "Show me the ideal size."

**6.** Wherever the hands stop is where the ideal size is.

**7.** Note if there was a difference between the actual size and the ideal size.

**8.** Was the ideal size the same, bigger, or smaller than the actual size?

Note that sometimes a field may be bigger than your arm span. In such cases, you can imagine working on a smaller scale, like when you imagined a smaller version of your body's biofield to clear it.

To adjust the size of a chakra to make it more active/bigger or less active/smaller, we will project energy into it. Our intention will be the factor that will determine whether the ray of white light we project will be increasing or decreasing the activity level.

We will be using a similar energizing/projecting technique as we did in the case of energizing depleted chakras.

## EXERCISE :: HARMONIZE A CHAKRA

Work with the same chakra that you just scanned or another clear chakra that you've determined would benefit from a size adjustment.

**1.** Scan again to get clear on whether the chakra would like to be bigger or smaller to match the ideal size. If no adjustment is required, keep scanning cleared chakras until you find one that could benefit from an adjustment.

**2.** Use the energy projecting technique: Imagine the chakra in front of you, receive universal energy, left palm upwards/right palm outwards, send a beam of light out of the projecting hand into the chakra, and circle the projecting/right hand clockwise as you intend to make the chakra bigger or smaller.

**3.** Scan again to see if the actual size is the same as the ideal size.
**4.** Add energy to make the chakra bigger or smaller as required.

Pro tip: If you accidentally make a chakra bigger than the ideal size you can always sweep some of the excess energy out of it.

Once you practice the harmonizing technique, you can try the variation below to see if you like it better.

### EXERCISE :: ALTERNATE HARMONIZING TECHNIQUE

**1.** Pick a chakra that has already been cleared.
**2.** Scan actual size.
**3.** Scan ideal size.
**4.** Note the difference and if an adjustment would be beneficial.
**5.** If an adjustment is indicated, go ahead with the next step. If not, keep scanning cleared chakras until you find one to adjust.
**6.** For this new energizing technique, bring your hands back to the actual size.
**7.** Holding both hands on either side, remembering to receive energy from source through your crown, send beams of light into the chakra from both of your hands simultaneously with an intention of making the chakra bigger or smaller, whatever is required.
**8.** Notice the feeling in your hands. You may feel the chakra change size.
**9.** Scan again to see if the chakra is at the ideal size and adjust as necessary.

I personally like this second technique, because my hands are already there and for me it is faster to energize out both hands, but it is very important when using two-handed energizing techniques to remember that you are still receiving energy and letting it flow through you. That is why it is recommended to focus on bringing energy in through the crown.

### EXERCISE :: HARMONIZE WITH INVOCATION

Practice balancing a chakra with an invocation instead of manually projecting energy:

**1.** Pick a chakra to work with.
**2.** Scan the chakra for energetic congestion and clear as needed. (**Chapter 8**)
**3.** Clear your hands.
**4.** Scan the chakra for energetic depletion and energize as needed.
**5.** Scan the actual size of the chakra.
**6.** Scan the ideal size of the chakra.
**7.** If there is a difference, use an invocation to adjust the size: "It is my intent that these chakras be energized for the purposes of balancing and harmonizing in the perfect way."
**8.** Scan again to check and see if the chakra is the ideal size.
**9.** Give thanks and clear your hands.


## HARMONIZING A CHANNEL

The central channel of the body's biofield can get congested, depleted, or underactive just like other parts of the energy body. As mentioned before, you can work with the central channel in three sections: the lower/Earth channel, the middle/core channel, and the upper/universal channel.

If a person's Earth channel is too small they can feel spaced-out, have trouble relaxing/sleeping, feel anxious, have physical symptoms of pain or illness, or any other symptoms related to being ungrounded.

If the universal channel is very big and the Earth channel is too small, a person may feel like an overloaded circuit with too much energy bouncing around or getting congested in the field. It can feel even more ungrounded than just having an under-active Earth channel on its own.

If the universal channel is too small, a person may feel cut-off from their spiritual guidance, separate/disconnected, depressed, apathetic, or confused. Anything related to being cut-off from universal intelligence.

In any of these cases, harmonizing the central channel will help bring welcome relief.

The first thing to do when working with the central channel is to clear it. After clearing the channel, energizing it if depleted, and sealing any possible leaks, you may find that the activity level or size of the channel could use an adjustment.

You determine this the same way you do for a chakra, by scanning the channel's actual size and ideal size. You can add energy in a similar way, too, by either using the receiving hand/projecting hand technique, or by projecting out both hands simultaneously.

Let's practice scanning and activating the Earth portion of the central channel. Follow the steps below.

## EXERCISE :: HARMONIZE THE EARTH CHANNEL

1. Invoke. (**Chapter 5**)
2. Cut cords. (**Chapter 6**)
3. Clear the Earth channel. (**Chapter 8**)
4. Clear your hands.
5. Scan the Earth channel to see its actual size.
6. Scan the ideal size of the Earth channel.
7. Was there a difference?
8. If so, set an intention to project energy to make the channel bigger or smaller, whichever is required.
9. Project energy into the channel by receiving from the universe, holding the receiving hand palm up and the projecting hand palm forward.
10. Send a beam of white light out of the projecting hand and into the channel.
11. Alternately, you could use the technique of projecting out both hands at once while receiving through the crown. Try both to see which one you like.
12. Scan the actual size again to see if it now matches the ideal size.
13. Adjust as necessary.
14. Scan again to check your work.

**15.** Give thanks and clear your space.

This technique can also be used for the other portions of the central channel: the universal channel above the crown and the core channel at the center of the body. Try it out.

As with the other energizing techniques in this chapter, you can alternately use an invocational technique to harmonize a channel. Simply scan the actual size and ideal size, and if there is a difference, invoke and state an intention that "this channel be harmonized in the perfect way."

## HARMONIZING THE BIOFIELD

Just like chakras and channels, sometimes the auric biofield of the body becomes unbalanced and could benefit from an adjustment. For example, if the biofield around someone's head is huge and the biofield around their lower chakras is small, they will tend to feel top-heavy energetically, like they are "in their heads" all the time and have difficulty connecting with their body. Harmonizing their biofield to bring more balancing energy to the lower part will facilitate feeling more connected to the body and help clear congestion from the overactive mental area.

To harmonize the biofield, we will be using a similar technique as before, just modified a bit.

## EXERCISE :: HARMONIZE THE BIOFIELD

**1.** Invoke. (**Chapter 5**)
**2.** Cut cords. (**Chapter 6**)
**3.** Clear the biofield. (**Chapter 7**)
**4.** Clear your hands.
**5.** Imagine the biofield in front of you again.
**6.** Scan the top part of the biofield to see what its actual size is.
**7.** Scan the middle part of the biofield to see what its actual size is.
**8.** Scan the bottom part of the biofield to see what its actual size is.

**9.** Notice if the biofield feels balanced top to bottom.
**10.** Scan the top, middle and bottom parts of the biofield for ideal size.
**11.** Notice if there is a difference between actual size and ideal size.
**12.** Adjust the size as necessary by projecting energy into a section of the biofield with the intention of making it bigger or smaller.
**13.** Scan again to check your work.
**14.** Give thanks and clear your hands.

There are many layers of the biofield, but you can affect all of them by having an intention to work on the overall biofield of the body. Having the biofield balanced also affects the fields within the field, like the chakras. Every little bit helps every other little bit.

And as mentioned before, you can alternately use an invocational technique to harmonize the biofield. Simply scan the actual size and ideal size, and if there is a difference, invoke and state an intention that, "This field be harmonized in the perfect way."

As if all those things weren't enough, there are even more amazingly practical and powerful uses of our energizing technique. In the next chapter, we'll look at some of them as well as how to close session. What? You mean we're almost to the end of the session protocol? Yes, indeed. You are about to graduate from this course. Give yourself a pat on the back.


## CHAPTER 9 :: KEY POINTS

• When energizing, always use transpersonal/universal energy.
• Be the clearest channel you can be.
• Clear energetic congestion before you energize to reduce the chance of body detox.
• Energy follows intention.
• Clear your hands before energizing.
• To channel universal energy effectively, breathe and relax.

## CHAPTER 9 :: INTEGRATION TIPS

• Bless/energize your food and water.
• Give energy to your houseplants. Scan to see if they'd like some first.
• Practice scanning and giving energy to garden plants and trees.
• If you have a pet you can give them energy, too. Just make sure you clear them first.
• Bless/energize the cells of your body by visualizing them filled with light.

## CHAPTER 9 :: PRACTICUM POSSIBILITIES

**Energizing/Blessing Food or Water:** (1 or 2 minutes)

You can send energy to your food or water to bless it.

**1.** For fun, scan the energy field of the food or water to see how big it is.
**2.** Invoke for clearing: "...it is my intent that this food/water be cleared in the perfect way."
**3.** Scan the field again to see if anything changed.
**4.** Use the receiving/projecting hand technique or the two hands projecting technique to project energy into the food/water and simultaneously invoke for charging/blessing: "...it is my intent that this food/water be blessed with love and gratitude."
**5.** Notice what you feel while blessing.
**6.** Scan the field of the food/water again. What happened?

You can use similar techniques to clear, charge and consecrate spaces, plants, medicine, crystals, you name it. Try it and see what happens. You may wish to note experiment results in your journal.

**Energizing with Imagination:** (in the moment)

As we have discovered in this course, our imaginations are powerful because our minds are powerful. For this experiment, I invite you to use your imagination throughout the day, whenever you think of it, to energize your body and its energy fields. Here are some ideas to get you started:

• Imagine your body filled with light and beaming in perfect, radiant health.
• Imagine your biofield is clear and filled with light.
• Imagine your channels clear and filled with light.
• Imagine your chakras clear and filled with light.
• Imagine the vision of what you're creating in your life clear and filled with light.

**Energizing on the Fly:** (in the moment)

The idea for this practice is that you can energize quickly with intention as you are going about your day, whenever you may feel it is required:

**1.** Notice if your body's energy feels ungrounded. (Are you running distracting mental loops, feeling anxious, spaced out?)
**2.** If you like, you can scan the size of your grounding/Earth channel.
**3.** Use an invocation to increase the size of your Earth channel: "It is my intent that my Earth channel be cleared, energized, strengthened, and balanced in the perfect way."
**4.** You can alternately command the Earth channel to activate or get bigger by saying, "Earth channel activate," or by imagining it getting bigger.

## The pinnacle

step by step
moment by moment

a practice is built
through the gift of time

had you rushed to the top
the air wouldn't sustain you

so, little by little
you built a foundation

to support you, sure-footed
on the path

day by day
you built trust and faith

in unconditional love
and your inevitable

ascension

# CHAPTER 10:
# SHIELDING +
# SEALING THE PROCESS

*Knowing it is done, we give thanks*

## COMPLETING SESSION WORK

In this chapter, we will learn the final steps of session work. We've learned how to work with our mind, how to invoke, cut cords, clear energy, and add energy. Now we will explore techniques for shielding the work we've done and sealing—or closing—the process of the session. We'll start with shields.

Shields are a subtle energetic form or intention we create to hold or protect an energy, space, or body. You can invoke that something be shielded, or you can create a psychic structure to shield it. There are many ways of shielding and many kinds of psychic structures. Different modalities focus on different things. In Lightworker Training, we'll practice both invocation and creating psychic structures for the purposes of shielding.

## PSYCHIC STRUCTURES

Psychic structures are things we can create to perform specific functions.

We create them with subtle energy and our intention. Some examples of psychic structures include:

• **Mirrors:** wall or shield-like structures for reflecting energy.

• **Cords:** intentional channel or rope-like structures created for binding or connecting energies.

• **Disposal units:** structures for disposing of unwanted energies, like a psychic fire or imaginary salt water bowl.

• **Containers:** structures for holding energy in or keeping energy out, such as shields, bubbles, spheres, circles, or boxes.

• **Generators:** structures for bringing energy in or clearing energy out, like vortices or pyramids.

• **Grids:** lines of energy for holding or activating energy of an intention or space.

• **Seals:** symbols used to protect a space or activate an energy, such as crosses, pentacles, geometric or Reiki symbols.

You could use almost any of these psychic structures for the purposes of shielding. For our practice, we will be working with a combination of three of them. We'll create a container that is a sphere of light. We will then add additional layers of mirrors and seals to our light sphere containers to make them even stronger.

## PRINCIPLES OF SHIELDING

Energetic shields are used for filtration or screening of energies and creating a space of protection. Similar to a bandage, the most safe and effective shields protect from infection while still being breathable.

In all the work we've done so far we have emphasized maintaining a lightness of heart and staying centered in love. Shielding is no exception. Remember that your true protection is in the remembrance of yourself as an eternal being of light that cannot be diminished or harmed in any way. Shields are for protection of spaces and fields of body. You are not your body. You don't need shields, but your body might require them for some time as it is healing.

It is not helpful to make shields from a mindset of fear and needing protection. But it is helpful to make shields to help keep an area clear. Can you feel the difference in the energy of those two intentions?

The shields we are making in this course are solid spheres or orbs of light, not membranes or bubbles. This means that the light of our shields will not only surround, but interpenetrate the area we are shielding. We make these shields to protect the work we have done, and to allow the body to integrate the new energy patterns without interference.

As with other forms of energizing, best practices indicate clearing before shielding. Ideally, the area you're shielding should be cleared of any cords, congestion, depletion, or leaks, and harmonized beforehand. There is a chance that the energy of the shield might have a side effect of resolving some of those things, but don't count on it. It's just as likely that adding energy into an uncleared area could cause a healing crisis reaction as described earlier.

That being said, if you feel a shield is required quickly, you can use an invocation to do it. You can either explicitly state an intention to clear congestion, resolve any depletion or leaks, harmonize, and then shield; or you can implicitly trust that when you download a shield from spirit, everything will be handled in the perfect way. Both approaches work.

Shields can be constructed for the biofield, the chakra fields or vortices, or specific areas of the body. You can also shield things like your home, a room therein, a pet, a car, you name it.

For our first shield, let's practice on a chakra.

## EXERCISE :: SHIELD A CHAKRA

**1.** Invoke. (**Chapter 5**)
**2.** Pick a chakra with which to work.
**3.** Cut cords. (**Chapter 6**)
**4.** Scan for congestion and clear manually or mentally. (**Chapter 8**)

**5.** Scan for depletion and energize as required. (**Chapter 9**)

**6.** Scan activity level and adjust as required. (**Chapter 9**)

**7.** Prepare to make a shield with the two-hand energizing technique by bringing your hands up in front of you, palms facing each other.

**8.** Focus on your crown and heart chakras as you project white light out both hands with the intention of creating a sphere of bright white light between them.

**9.** Imagine that sphere of white light growing stronger between your hands.

**10.** After a few breaths, or whenever you feel the sphere between your hands is big enough, imagine that there is a fine metallic silver sheen or sparkle all throughout the white light.

**11.** Imagine or intend that every tiny particle of that silver dust is a magical symbol that is magnetizing supportive, positive energy into the field, and repelling any toxic, negative energy out of the field.

**12.** Install the shield by imagining you are placing the silver-white sphere of light around the chakra and that the silver-white light also interpenetrates the chakra.

**13.** While holding it there, program the shield by invoking, "It is my intent that this chakra be shielded in the perfect way for the perfect amount of time."

**14.** Give thanks and clear your space.

The tiny silver symbols are the seals that strengthen the shield. You may see what the symbols are or not. You may intentionally choose a specific symbol or not. Either way works because the energy will follow your intention whether you are aware of the outcome or not. I like to invoke seals and just see what shows up. Experiment to see what works for you.

The silver sheen or silvery dusting in the sphere of light provides some of the reflecting energy of a mirror without the negative side effects of energy boomeranging back on people who might be projecting unloving thoughts your way.

After shielding, you may like to scan to see how strong the shield is and for how many days it will last. As you get stronger in your practice, your shields will last longer.

Remember, when working with chakras you have a choice to work with the whole field of the chakra or to work the front and back vortices individually. So, when it comes to shielding, you may choose to make one shield that encompasses the whole chakral field or you can choose to make a shield for each vortex. If you only clear one vortex, or side, of a chakra then it is best to shield only the side that you worked on. For example, if you only cleared the front solar plexus chakra, just shield the front.

## SHIELDING THE BIOFIELD

As a general guideline, when clearing, it is usually more helpful to work from outside in, or from more general field clearing to more specific local clearing, which is exactly what we've already been doing. We started with clearing the biofield and then moved in to more specific clearing in chakras. With energizing, especially in the form of shielding, it is usually more helpful to work from inside out, shielding chakras first and then moving out to shield the auric biofield.

## EXERCISE :: SHIELD THE BIOFIELD

**1.** Invoke. (**Chapter 5**)
**2.** Cut cords on the biofield, front and back. (**Chapter 6**)
**3.** Sweep congestion out of the biofield. (**Chapter 7**)
**4.** Energize depletion or leaks as required. (**Chapter 9**)
**5.** Scan activity level and adjust as required. (**Chapter 9**)
**6.** Prepare to make a shield with the two-hand energizing technique by bringing your hands up in front of you, palms facing each other.
**7.** Focus on your crown and heart as you project energy out both hands with the intention of creating a sphere of bright white light between them.
**8.** Imagine a sphere of white light growing between your hands.
**9.** After a few breaths, or whenever you feel the sphere between your hands is big enough, imagine that there is a fine metallic silver sheen throughout the white light.
**10.** Imagine or intend that every tiny particle of that silver dust is a magical symbol that is magnetizing supportive, positive energy into the field, and

repelling any toxic, negative energy out of the field.

**11.** Install the shield by imagining you are placing the silver-white sphere of light around the biofield and that the silver-white light also interpenetrates the field.

**12.** While holding it there, program the shield by invoking: "It is my intent that this biofield be shielded in the perfect way for the perfect amount of time."

**13.** Give thanks and clear your space.

If you feel intuitively guided to add another element of intention to the shield, you can use the invocation to adjust the programming. For example, you may wish to add another shield specifically for the emotional body, in which case you could install another shield and invoke: "It is my intent that the emotional body be shielded in the perfect way for the perfect amount of time."

If you are shielding and the universe gives you a download of a specific frequency to use in the shield, like the energy of a crystal, flower, or color, you can go with your intuition. Remember, messages from source consciousness always feel light, loving and peaceful. You can trust in that. If you're unsure, you can ask your body as described in Chapter 6, or scan for confirmation.

If, however, you are in your analytical ego mind and are trying to figure out a fancy shield frequency, it would be more beneficial to keep your intention simple and allow spirit to add anything that may be required.

## SEALING THE PROCESS OF SESSION WORK

When performing a lightwork session, or any portion of a full session, it is important to close down the process as mindfully as you opened it. There are a few simple but important steps to take to ensure that the session is complete:

- Check in.
- Invoke for completion.

- Give thanks.
- Release the energy.
- Clear your space.

Most of this you know intuitively and have been practicing already, but let's break down each step a bit to see what it entails and why it is helpful.

## CHECK IN

When you're coming to the close of a session and starting to feel complete, it is important to check in with yourself, with the other person with whom you're working, and with spirit to see if the process is complete or if there is something still up for healing in this session.

Sometimes when the energies have been shifting, it may be necessary to go back to an area you already cleared because another layer has arisen for clearing. This is great. It means you unlocked something that allowed for even deeper healing. What it does *not* mean is that you did a crappy job of clearing it the first time.

Sometimes when energy that has been previously blocked starts flowing again, it can hit congestion in another area of the body that hasn't been cleared yet. When that happens, the energy can start to build up pressure, which may feel uncomfortable. If you are working on yourself, you will probably notice it. If you are working with someone else, you may not catch it, so it's important to check in with them by asking if there's anything else coming up, anything that could use some clearing. I usually say something to the client like, "Notice what's happening in the body now. Is there anything you notice that is asking for some more attention, or are you feeling complete for today?"

If something comes up, you can go to that area and clear congestion, either manually by sweeping or mentally through invocation. You can also energize, harmonize or shield either manually or mentally.

When I am coming to the end of a session, I check in with spirit to see if there is anything else for us to do. If I get a "yes," I open to receive the information of what that might be. If I don't seem to get a clear answer, I scan through the field mentally or manually until my attention or hand stops wherever the issue is, then we clear it. I continue to ask if there is anything else to do until I get a "no," then I check in with the client to see if anything is coming up for them, and continue to clear until they feel complete.

What if you can't tell if there's something else? Or what if you ask and so much comes up that it feels overwhelming?

Let me give you a clue:

## INVOKE FOR COMPLETION

Just like we open session intentionally with a prayer or invocation, we close it the same way. In the opening, we are focused on the intention that whatever comes up for healing be released and whatever energies are required to balance be received in the most graceful way. In closing a session, the intention is focused more on gratitude for all that has unfolded and completion of anything else that is required.

Invoking for completion is a way to make sure we don't leave anything important undone. Here's a simple invocation for completion of a session:

*"It is my intent that anything else required for this session be released or received in the perfect way now."*

We are often working within some kind of time container, like a 20-minute practice period or an hour-long session. If you start with a focused intention, that helps keep the work within the time boundary. For example, choosing to focus on the main issue, or one specific thing, rather than whatever comes up will help focus your efforts. You can also be mindful of the time and adjust methods to suit time availability. Invocation tends to go faster, manual techniques tend to go slower.

When you are noticing that the end of your session time is growing near, start checking in, tying up any loose ends, and invoking for completion. It is helpful to allow a bit of processing and transition time at the end, too. As you practice, you will become more adept at knowing how long it usually takes you for each one of these things.

## GIVE THANKS

Just as gratitude is a key component of the smaller processes of invocations, it is also key for the larger process of session work. We give thanks knowing that the work is done.

The most important element of giving thanks is the feeling of gratitude. That might seem obvious at first, but try this:

**1.** Think the phrase "thank you" in your mind.
**2.** Now, pause, take a breath, and feel "thank you" in your heart.
**3.** Notice the difference.

When giving thanks before, during, or after session, the key to a powerful practice is the feeling in your heart, so take a breath and feel the perfection of the work, the joy of a job well done, the honor of having the opportunity to do the work, and the gratitude for all the help you have.

It's not complicated. It doesn't take a lot of time. But it is essential.

A closing prayer is really a celebration. The more you feel that energy of deep gratitude and joy, the more effective your work will be.

When I'm working, I'm affirming accomplishment, unity, and gratitude the whole time. At the end of session, I reaffirm it by saying a prayer of gratitude silently or aloud. Here is a typical closing prayer for me:

*"We give thanks for love light consciousness flowing through us and through all things; so grateful that we never do this or anything alone. We're grateful to receive this healing on the deepest level and in the perfect way; grateful to share the benefits with everyone; grateful to let it be and so it is."*

**RELEASE THE ENERGY**

When session is complete, it is important to release the energy by cutting any cords to the person with whom you're working and your attachment to the outcome.

Sometimes when we are sourcing energy for session work, we will unintentionally create a psychic structure like an umbilical cord of energy from us to our client. If we don't cut it, that person may continue receiving energy from us even though we aren't consciously sourcing, which will result in draining our body's personal energy reserves. We may also end up unconsciously taking back some of the energy that was intended for the other person.

It is equally important to cut the cord of the attachment to the outcome of the work you just did. This is true whether you are working with another person or yourself. By cutting the cord of attachment to the outcome, we release our ideas about what a good or bad healing result is. We release attachment to being a good or bad healer. We release our need for recognition or affirmation. We give all the burden and gratitude of the work to spirit and we practice trusting that it is done for us.

Any time I find myself even thinking, let alone worrying, about a client or a session, I cut the cord again and I give thanks that I'm not doing the work, spirit is.


**CLEAR YOUR SPACE**

Once we check in, invoke to complete, give thanks, and release attachments, we are ready to clear ourselves and our space of any residual energies from the session. You can do this mentally with an invocation or visualization. You can do it manually by sweeping your body and your space. You can clear with a smudge spray, burning some incense, toning, ringing bells or playing singing bowls. It can be as simple as imagining everything infused with light.

I typically use a combination of invocation/visualization, smudge spray, and sweeping. Whether I'm in an in-person session or remote session, after the client leaves or we hang up, I clear myself and the space again. I clear any furnishings, too, like the couch, chair, massage table, blankets, pillows, and bolsters.

If you build effective energy hygiene into your routine you will continue to work more and more clearly and powerfully without energy drain and burn-out. Anytime you feel off, tired, or cranky, check and see if you picked up some energy or entity and use the invocation to clear it out of your space, because holding on to that is not helpful for anyone.

## EXERCISE :: SEAL THE PROCESS

Now that we are clear on the steps of closing a session, let's practice to get a feeling for it. Use this to close out what you've already been working on from this chapter, or if you are coming to the practice after taking a break, start a new session.

**1.** Invoke.
**2.** Do a mini session for yourself, or continue with the process from shielding practice earlier in this chapter.
**3.** Check in to see if there is anything else coming up for healing at this time.
**4.** If you get a "yes" keep working until you get a "no" or use invocation to complete the session.
**5.** Say a prayer of gratitude that the work is done in the perfect way.
**6.** Cut cords to the session and outcome.
**7.** Clear your body and your space of any residual energies.

Often I will spend a little time talking to a client after session is over, so after they leave I will cut cords again. If I happen to think about a client after that, I'll scan for cords. Cords to clients can attach at any time, even if you're not currently working with them.

Whether you're working on yourself or someone else, if you think about the work with attachment to the outcome afterward like, "I hope they enjoyed the session," or, "I hope I actually cleared that thing," or, "I hope they feel better," or, "I don't know if I did that right," or anything like that, scan and cut cords.

It is vital to maintain mental focus on the work being done perfectly. Remember, every thought is creative and worry is a prayer for what you don't want, so cut cords, say a prayer of gratitude that your ego isn't the one doing the work, or whatever it takes to be in the energy of non-attachment. And as we know, non-attachment is essential for good energy hygiene.

Another thing that helps maintain good energy hygiene is staying grounded and embodied. You can stay grounded by activating and strengthening your Earth channel. You can stay embodied by being present and noticing what's happening in your body. If the light of your consciousness is filling your body completely, there's no room for shady energies to move in.

As you go through session work, keep checking in with your body and your grounding, and you won't get entangled with the energies you're clearing. In fact, once you master being grounded, fully embodied, and non-attached, your body won't require shields any more.

Congratulations! You now have an understanding and practice of all the basic components of a full lightwork session. Take some time this week to practice a complete session for yourself and celebrate.

Receiving this toolkit is just the first step, so practice, have fun, and notice if you feel lighter and lighter as you go. If anything comes up that feels overwhelming or confusing, hand it over to spirit.

Remember, you always have access to the perfect assistance of infinite consciousness and you can create possibilities outside the limitations of your perceived reality.

## CHAPTER 10 :: KEY POINTS

- Shields are for finite bodies, not infinite beings.
- Your true safety is in knowing your essence is eternal and all is well.
- Shields are a kind of psychic structure.
- Shields are helpful to maintain a space for healing energy to integrate.
- Shields are like an energetic bandage.
- Sealing the process ensures perfect completion of session work.
- The most important element of prayer is a feeling of gratitude.
- Cutting cords helps release attachment to the outcome of session work.
- Keeping your self and your space clear is essential energetic hygiene.

## CHAPTER 10 :: INTEGRATION TIPS

- Invoke to clear and shield yourself before going to work at the beginning of the day.
- Invoke to clear and shield yourself before going to bed at the end of the day.
- Invoke to clear and shield a project you're working on from other people's projections.
- Invoke to clear and shield the healing space you're doing session work in.

## CHAPTER 10 :: PRACTICUM POSSIBILITIES

**Practice a Complete Lightwork Session:** (up to 60 minutes)

Now that you've got all the tools, it's time to put them together in a complete session for yourself.

For this practice, take some time with your Lightwork Session Protocol outline from the **Appendix** and go through it, step by step, practicing each of the techniques in the order given.

Use the **Chakra Chart** as a reminder as needed as well as your notes or book. It's totally cool to use your notes during session. There are master healers who use books while working. The more you practice the steps, the faster you will learn them and the sooner you will be able to remember them all without notes. Once you understand the reasoning behind the system, the process of session work is actually very intuitive.

It is beneficial to practice the Lightwork Session Protocol separately from other modalities you may use until you are thoroughly comfortable with it. Once it is clear in your mind, you can add other modalities and blend it intuitively into your healing practice. This is something that is recommended with all new modalities you acquire. Take the time to practice only the new modality from beginning to end. You can have other practice periods that combine modalities, but to really master a technique it is important to have time dedicated to just that.

As you practice, you may wish to make notes on what arises in session. The more you put into your practice, the more you will get out of it. It doesn't require long practice periods, but it does require some quality, focused time on a regular basis to master the skills.

Now get in there and have fun with your session!

**Practice Shielding a Space:** (10 minutes)

For this practice, we will explore creating shields for spaces that are not part of your body. Let's start with the area around your bed. This will be great for helping you get a better night's sleep.

**1. Clear the space:** With any shield it is helpful to clear first. You could sweep the bed area manually either in real time/space or remotely (imagining a mini bed) or you could use the invocation, "It is my intent that my bed and the area around my bed be cleared now."

**2. Build and install the shield:** You could do this manually by remotely shielding as described earlier this chapter or you could do it mentally by visualizing the shield around the bed.

**3. Program the shield**: To program the shield, invoke, "It is my intent that my bed and the area around my bed be shielded in the perfect way for the perfect amount of time."

You can use this same technique to shield a room in a house, or the whole house. Same with apartments. You can do a room, the apartment, or the whole building. I find it most helpful to use the invocation for big jobs like that. I'm guessing you probably don't want to manually clear a whole building.

My favorite technique for shielding my bedroom at night is to shield my body, then put up a shield around my bed, then around the bedroom, then the whole apartment, then the whole house, then the whole property. So, it's like the Russian nesting dolls, shields within shields within shields.

Practice with different levels of shielding to see what is most helpful. It may seem like all those layers are a lot of work, but as you practice you will get faster and your shields will last longer. I find that a lot of layers help keep my spirit from running around all over the multiverse while I'm sleeping and I feel more rested in the morning.

**Expand into space**


you are the light
of stars

and the space
in between

the connection of
constellations

the infinite possibilities
of consciousness evolving

shockwave enlightenment
ripples out to eternity

expanding unbounded
awakening

circles within circles
revolutionary love songs

echoing through
the one mind we share

# CHAPTER 11:
# ADDITIONAL EXPLORATIONS

*In the spiral of life, every ending is a beginning*

## WHAT ELSE IS POSSIBLE?

Through practicing the concepts we grasp intellectually, we have an embodied experience of knowing it. The more we have those moments of knowing, the stronger our faith in ourselves and in our connection to the infinite consciousness that guides and sustains everything in the multiverse.

Although this chapter concludes the lessons of this manual, it is the beginning of the continuing education and development of your lightwork skills. The cool thing about the foundational skills you've learned is that they have infinite applications.

In this chapter we'll explore just a bit of what else is possible with lightwork. We'll be looking at how to hold space as a healer, healing addiction, clearing entities, psychic attack and defense, clearing spaces, working with crystals, and self care.

## HOLDING SPACE AS A HEALER

Just as the only true safety we have is in identification as spirit and oneness, the only true power to heal comes from that same source of unity consciousness. When someone comes to you asking for help and healing, the most helpful thing you can do is to focus the power of your consciousness on their inherently perfect spirit.

The most effective way of holding space for healing is to affirm that the person you are working with is already free, already perfect, and already a powerful co-creator of their reality. Focusing on thoughts of their apparent lack or limitation is not helpful. So, even as you are working on clearing blocks or diseased energy in their field, it is crucial to hold in your mind their perfect state of health and wellness that already exists.

It may be helpful to think of yourself as connecting two states of being. One is the current state of seeming unwell. The other is the future state of perfect health. You are bringing the energy of the future state into the current moment in time. If you focus on the future state wellness already being here, that will prevail because that is your intent and that is the truth.

The only reason we don't experience abundant health, joy, and wellness is because of our blocks to receiving those energies. Our blocks come in the form of things like our beliefs, old trauma, trapped emotions, and all the energetic congestion that stems from them. You don't have to know exactly what the block is, you can simply invoke or intend to clear the blocks to wellness.

The following list gives important points to remember when holding space for healing. Take time to read through them, pausing after each one to contemplate what that feels like for you. Notice which ones really land with you. Notice which ones spark a feeling of inquiry. Notice which ones feel like a stretch to believe.

- Love is the healer and you are love.
- Everyone is already perfect.
- There is nothing that needs fixing or doing.

- There is no right/wrong/good/bad.
- Everything is simply a choice.
- Everything is for our learning.
- What heals one heals all.
- The separation never happened.
- We are one with everything in nature.
- In the oneness lies all power, safety, and knowledge.
- When we are identified as separate we cannot heal or be helpful.
- When we remember that we are one with the infinite mind we tap into infinite possibilities.
- When we choose to think loving thoughts we will experience healing.

If it feels helpful, take a moment to write down any reflections.

If we could truly be the energy, space, and consciousness of the key points listed above, we probably wouldn't need any of the other tools in this book. The ultimate way to hold space as a healer is to be the embodiment of what is truly healing.

When we hold space as a healer, we bridge heaven and earth. We focus on divine order in the midst of chaos. We choose our light and power in the darkest circumstances. We inhabit the space of knowing that we are merely a speck of dust in the infinite universe and that we are so absolutely precious that the infinite universe would be incomplete without us. These things only appear to be incompatible to our egos. If we approach our work with humility and power, without attachment but with perfect trust, lightly yet sincerely, we will be successful.

As with any other skill we're developing, we must practice holding space in order to master it. As you go, you will have the pleasure of discovering beautiful refinements. And you will no doubt remember again and again that you are only ever healing yourself. There is no one else to heal.

## HEALING ADDICTION

Something that comes up a lot in session is the energy of addiction and what we think of as bad habits. I've yet to meet anyone who doesn't have some kind of addictive behavior with which they struggle.

The capitalist culture we are immersed in is geared toward distraction, disempowerment, and consumption. It thrives off selling us stuff that contributes to our tendency for addictive escapism. It is also a culture of externalization and projection, so it has taught us that external things are the causes of all of our pleasure and pain. If the cause of our addictions were things like drugs, alcohol, gambling, and sex, simply quitting the behavior or substance would cure it, but it doesn't, because addiction starts in the mind.

Addiction starts as an idea that you're not okay in this moment. That something is wrong or lacking. The seed idea is usually planted in a traumatizing situation and instead of getting healed, it grows. The more trauma one has encountered in life, especially in childhood, the more challenging it is to dig out the roots of addiction, but it can be done.

The truth is, anyone can get addicted to anything. Our bodies have chemical responses to internal and external stimuli, and we can get addicted to those chemicals. We can get addicted to thought patterns that evoke a certain emotional response, which trigger a physical chemical response.

How many times a day—or an hour—do you compulsively check your phone, looking for that little bump in happy brain chemicals? How many times do you not give yourself enough time so that you get a rush of adrenaline from running late? How many times do you stress yourself out to get a cortisol spike?

Some folks have a hard time functioning if they're not rushing around stressed out. The adrenaline and cortisol from stress and anxiety are fueling their productivity as much, if not more than, their caffeine consumption.

Thankfully, we can get free of these patterns. If you struggle with an addictive habit, you can get free with the tools in your lightworker kit. As we have learned, the key to changing anything is the mindset of willingness. Once you have that, you can implement some strategies and techniques.

Before an addiction trigger strikes, decide ahead of time what the plan is.

Here's a simple one:

**1.** Notice that you are triggered.
**2.** Get present.
**3.** Breathe.
**4.** Notice what you feel in your body.
**5.** Breathe some more.

That probably sounds familiar by now. And in fact, if you are healing addiction, you might find it very helpful to go back and read **Chapter 2: Foundations of Healing** through the perspective of healing addiction.

Most addictive behaviors are coping mechanisms that have become unhelpful ways of dealing with the challenges of life. Have compassion for yourself and understand that the part of you that is hooked into this addictive pattern is a wounded part of you that is crying for love. Love will ultimately heal whatever the root cause of the addiction is, but in the meantime, you might like to employ strategies for deprogramming yourself from your habit.

Here's another technique, like getting present, that really helped me. As you may recall from what I've shared about myself, I struggled with different forms of behavioral and chemical addictions throughout my life. The following strategy is something I thought up when I was working on avoiding yet another relapse into heroin dependency:

**1.** Personify the addiction.
**2.** Imagine it as an actual entity.
**3.** Remember the entity is doing its best to stay alive no matter what.

I thought of my addiction entity as a spider in my brain. The spider sounded like my thoughts because it was hooked into my brain, but it wasn't me. I figured out a way of discerning what was my thought and what was the spider's. It was simple: every time I had a thought about doing dope, it was the spider. Because, you see, I had already decided that I didn't want to do it any more, so it wasn't me who said, "Just this once." It was the thing I was starving out who was desperately trying to get me to feed it. It was tricky, but I was trickier.

It worked like a charm. Quitting was still challenging, but the moment I realized that the addictive thoughts weren't mine, I had a consciousness tool that changed the game forever. I use similar ideas for other voices that pop up in my mind, like the ego, the critic, or other people's judgments. I remind myself that that's not really me.

Another thing that is important to know about changing any habit is that it takes time and focus. To be successful, focus on one thing at a time. Don't try to change everything at once. Trust me, changing one deeply ingrained habit is enough to do at any one time. Once that becomes the new normal, then think about the next thing.

If you have a pattern you're struggling to undo, a habit that causes you pain, or a compulsive behavior that you feel is taking up too much space in your life, I invite you to try this technique: have a plan, be present when you're triggered, personify your demons, and take it one step at a time.

See for yourself how powerful it can be. See how powerful you can be when you're not identified as your addiction.

## A WORD ON DEMONS + ENTITIES

The interesting thing about the spider personification I imagined back in the day is that it's a surprisingly accurate description of some of the entities I now see everyday in my work and in the world. Yep, there are some pretty bizarre looking entities out there. If you see one, you might get freaked out, but please know there is no need to fear. In fact, if there is a need, it is to not fear.

As common sense would dictate, if you encounter an entity that feeds off fear and you are afraid of it, you won't be able to clear it. You also can't clear something with which you are entangled. As we learned in **Chap-**

**ter 6: Scanning Energies + Cord Cutting**, we get energetically corded to things through our judgments. When clearing entities we must maintain non-judgment of the entity, of having the entity, and of not having the entity. If you have attachment to having or not having entities, you won't be able to clear them. Fortunately, we have tools for clearing cords of attachment.

Take a moment now to scan and cut any cords you may have to entities, to thoughts of entities, or to clearing entities.

...............................................

Entities are organisms made of subtle energy. They come in all different sizes and forms, just like organisms in the denser energy of the physical world. Entities are all around us all the time. Like any being that wants to survive, they get attracted to their food sources. If you are holding or emitting the frequency of the energy a certain entity feeds off of, it will be attracted to you. If you feed it, it will stick around and keep demanding more food. If you know what energy an entity is attracted to, you can use invocation to clear that specific energy, or use invocation to clear "whatever energy is attracting these entities."

*Demon* is a term given to a certain kind of entity that will take over part of our mind or body if we're not interested in being conscious. In a sense, demons do jobs for us. They help us be unconscious in some area of our lives. Because our natural state of being is conscious, we have to get help to be unconscious. Demons aren't really that big of a deal. The trickiest thing about clearing them is the tendency to go unconscious when engaging their energy. If you are doing a clearing and you start feeling distracted or can't seem to focus, you're probably hitting up on some demon energy. As a matter of fact, there's a good chance that just by reading this paragraph something is getting triggered, so let's do this:

*"I am thankful to be joined in my heart and mind with the one heart, the one mind of creation. I am thankful and grateful to be clearing any and all demons and entities through any and all dimensions of time and space, from any and*

*all of my many bodies now. Anything that doesn't allow that, I am also clearing completely and permanently. I am thankful to let it be and so it is."*

Take a breath and read or say it again with feeling.

Remember, anything that comes up for clearing, no matter how weird, no matter how crazy it makes you feel, you can clear it, because you have the tool of invocation. (And because you're awesome like that.) Your true nature is one of light, love, and power, so you are destined to be free.

Focusing on your true nature is not only essential when dealing with entities, but also when dealing with the energy of psychic attack.

## PSYCHIC SELF-DEFENSE

*Psychic self-defense* is knowing how to effectively deal with the energy of psychic attack. Simply put: psychic attack is an unloving thought. Whenever you perceive the energy of psychic attack, you are sensing unloving thoughts. Many times these will seem to be your thoughts. They may appear as unloving thoughts you have about yourself or someone else. You may notice that you are attacking or defending yourself or another person in your mind. Whether the energy of attack appears to be coming from inside or outside doesn't matter. You can deal with it in the same way:

Recognize that you are the only one who has given this attack power and you can take that power away any time you choose.

Because the power of our minds is the power of the consciousness of creation, it benefits us to be mindful of what beliefs we energize. If you buy into belief in attack, the power of your mind will energize that belief and you will experience the effect of feeling attacked. If you attack (think an unloving thought about) someone else, you will be demonstrating your belief in attack and you will also feel attacked.

When you feel attacked, the most helpful thing you can do is to invoke to clear the belief in attack and then clear the energy. It is not helpful to tell stories about it, run scenarios of "what if," launch a counteroffensive, or energize a fearful belief in the need for protection. Simply invoke, clear any ego/fear-based beliefs, clear the negative energy from your field, shield yourself up, and be grateful that spirit's got your back.

When you are partnered up with the infinite mind, nothing is stronger than you because you are affirming unity and tapping into the power of all that is. No hateful thought, no curse or demon is stronger than that.

When you feel like you're being attacked psychically, your body might be going into the sympathetic survival mode of fight or flight. In which case, it will be helpful to take steps to switch into a parasympathetic state. The way to do that is to take deep breaths and feel what's happening in your body until it calms down. Once you come out of survival mode, you'll be able to think clearly and deal with whatever is arising effectively.

When it comes to physical self-defense, the best defense is a good offense, but in energy and consciousness, the best defense is being un-offendable. That means releasing all the judgments, stories, and meanings about the attack.

It can be tricky to maintain non-judgment when you feel attacked, but let's be clear: you as an infinite being cannot be attacked. Your body can be, but you are not your body. To transcend the energy of attack, we must release all belief in attack and attachment to that belief.

If the body is being attacked, that's a different story. In that case, fight or flight is helpful, but when it comes to psychic attack, we are dealing with the mental level, also known as the causal level, so we must focus energy on the *effect we'd like to achieve.*

When we activate causal thoughts that affirm the reality and power of attack, we will experience the effects/feelings of being attacked. If we'd like to experience the feeling of being impervious to attack, we must energize thoughts of its lack of power over us.

The only way attack energy will stick in our field is if we align with it or fight against it. Both are forms of attachment. In the section **Energy Hygiene** in **Chapter 7: Energy Hygiene + Biofield Clearing** we looked at the importance of releasing attachment and maintaining a lovingly neutral state of mind, even going so far as trusting that on some level there is a perfection inherent in everything.

When you notice someone sending unloving thoughts your way, you can remain neutral and see it not as an attack on you, but as someone having unloving thoughts about themselves that they are attempting to project onto you. You do not have to accept those projections as real or as having any power over you. However you approach it, this mindset of neutrality is essential in clearing energies and maintaining energetic hygiene.

Remember, being loving doesn't mean having crappy boundaries and letting people abuse you or your body. Sometimes the most loving thing is kicking ass. Think about how nature operates. It doesn't judge anything. It doesn't make meaning out of it or tell stories or form attachments.

As we've learned, if you energize your attachments to something, you will not be able to effectively clear it or stay clear of it because you have created a cord of energy to it. Makes sense, right?

Now that we've got the principles down, lets break down the process for clearing psychic attack:

## EXERCISE :: CLEAR PSYCHIC ATTACK

**1.** Invoke. (**Chapter 5**)
**2.** Affirm that you are spirit, nothing can harm you, and you are one with all that is.
**3.** Release attachments by cutting cords on the biofield and chakras. (**Chapter 6**)
**4.** Invoke to clear any belief in attack by saying, "It is my intent to clear any and all beliefs in separation, lack, attack, and limitation through all dimensions of time and space."
**5.** Invoke to clear any negative energies from your field: "It is my intent to

clear any and all negative energies and entities from my many bodies now and anything that doesn't allow that, dissolve and resolve back to the root cause now."

**6.** Invoke for completion: "It is my intent that anything else that is required for permanent clearing of this energy or any replacement energies that are required for the balancing of my many fields and bodies be received on whatever level is required now."

**7.** Invoke to shield: "It is my intent that my many fields and bodies be shielded in the perfect way for the perfect amount of time."

**8.** Give thanks.

**9.** Cut the cord to your work and attachment to the outcome.

**10.** Clear your space.

If you feel you could use some extra assistance, remember that you have a whole squad of spiritual guides and helpers that can surround and support you.

The most helpful thing to remember about psychic attack is that you can transcend the energy of attack by rising above the battlefield. If you are willing to release all of your unloving thoughts and keep working that energy, you will rise higher and higher in your vibration. This is helpful because there is no safety in a battlefield. There is no safety in lack, attack, limitation, and separation. The only true safety there is comes in knowing yourself and all kindred beings as spirit, perfect and holy.

## CLEARING SPACES

You can use what you know about clearing the energy body and physical body tissues to clear spaces or things in your home. Just like the other clearing techniques we've learned, there are mental ways and manual ways of doing the work. For both it can be helpful to use your scanning technique to get a read on the energy before, during, and after.

Let's start with practicing the mental technique on a room in your house:

## EXERCISE :: CLEAR A SPACE

**1.** Scan the energy of the room you'd like to clear to see how much energetic congestion there is. You can also scan for more specific energies.

**2.** Use the invocation to clear, "It is my intent to clear any and all energetic congestion (or toxic/harmful energy or entities) in this space all the way back to the root cause."

**3.** Scan again to see if there is any of that energy left (it might take a little time to clear).

**4.** If there is a portion that is not clearing, use the invocation, "It is my intent to clear anything that doesn't allow this energy to clear completely and permanently."

**5.** Scan again and keep changing up the invocation as needed until the energy is clear.

For manual clearing of a space you could use your big hands of light, but even with very large hands it would be a lot of sweeping to clear a large room or a house. For clearing a big space manually, I like to use a tool called Walls of Light.

## EXERCISE :: WALLS OF LIGHT

For this practice, I will describe a physical technique, but you can also perform it in your mind.

**1.** Start by invoking for assistance.

**2.** Begin the sweep by standing at the edge of the room with your back to the wall and your hands, palms facing forward, held out a bit in front of you.

**3.** Imagine that in front of you is a wall of light that your palms are touching. The wall is made of brilliant light and is about two feet thick. This wall extends all the way through the building's structure and out past the edges of it in four directions, down into the earth, up into the sky, and out to either side.

**4.** Once you have the wall of light established, begin to slowly push the wall through the space by walking forward. If it is hitting a lot of congestion and moving very slowly, imagine you have your entire spirit squad assisting you. Many hands make light work. (Light work. Get it?)

**5.** Keep walking forward and pushing the wall of light through the room, noticing what it feels like as you go, until you get to the other side of the room.

**6.** At the edge of the room, imagine you are pushing the Wall of Light all the way through the wall, through the whole building and out into space. You don't have to worry about where the congestion is going because the light is actually dissolving it, but you can send it all into the sun if that feels better.

**7.** Now that you've completed one pass through the room, turn around repeat the process so that you are passing through the room in the other direction.

**8.** When you get to the end of the room, push the wall of light out to space like you did before.

**9.** Repeat going back in the other direction, walking through and pushing the Wall of Light out into space at the end.

**10.** Turn and repeat one more time.

**11.** Now that you have been through the space four times, notice if it seems to be getting clearer.

**12.** Keep passing through the space with walls of light until it feels like you're not hitting any congestion, or until a scan shows no more congestion.

Pro tip: You can also work this tool remotely by imagining a small version of the room or building in front of you and sweeping walls of light through it.

When practicing clearing spaces, try both the manual and mental techniques combined with scanning. Perhaps you will discover creative combinations like invoking for the Walls of Light process to run without doing it manually.

As mentioned in the section on shielding, you can shield spaces as well as fields of the energy body. Once you've worked the above tools to clear a space, practice shielding it as well to help keep the energy clearer for longer periods of time. See the practicum section of **Chapter 10: Shielding +**

**Sealing The Process** for a description of that technique.


## WORKING WITH CRYSTALS

Crystals are healing allies from the mineral kingdom. Many people are drawn to working with them due to their beauty and energy. You can use what you know about lightwork techniques and apply it to working with crystals. Diving deep into crystal healing techniques is beyond the scope of this book, but we will look at ways to understand and care for crystals. It is important to understand the basic nature of crystals so that you can work with them mindfully.

Crystals have consciousness just like everything in the universe. Their consciousness does not appear to be as complex as ours, but they do embody a kind of intelligence. Crystals naturally absorb, condense, store, and emit energy. They are nature's batteries. They have the ability to follow simple instructions, so they are programmable. They also have a tendency to activate energy fields like chakras.

These physical and energetic qualities are the ways in which all crystals naturally function. No matter what kind of crystal, it will naturally do the following:

- Absorb energy
- Condense energy
- Store energy
- Emit energy
- Receive imprints/programs
- Activate fields

Because of their natural ability to absorb and store, crystals tend to pick up a lot of random energies. And because they naturally emit energy, too, they will project—and even amplify—the random energies they've picked up. As you can imagine, sometimes this is not helpful.

Another quality of crystals is the ability to activate energy, especially the energy fields of our bodies. This can be helpful, but only if the field requires further activation and if the energies being activated are indicated for that particular application. Specific applications are beyond the scope of this manual, but we can learn some general guidelines and practice some tools.

As a general rule of thumb, because crystals are always activating, having them around is contraindicated in cases of overactivity. Examples of things we don't want to further activate include: viral outbreaks, cancerous cell growth, hyperactivity, hypertension, psychosis, and high blood pressure. If you have anxiety or insomnia, I recommend removing all crystals from your bedroom, especially diamond jewelry. Diamonds are extremely powerful crystals. Most crystals are also contraindicated for pregnancy, so when in doubt, leave it out.

Colored crystals work on the color rays, which are very potent. Adding crystal energy to color energy makes it even more powerful. This is great if you are aware of the properties of the colors and crystals, their effects and their contraindications. Not so great if you don't know. Luckily, we have our scanning tool, so anytime you'd like to know if a crystal is safe and effective for a particular application, you can scan for the amount of safety and effectiveness. Ask your body (as described in Chapter 6) if it would like to wear a certain crystal. After wearing it for a while, ask your body if it still wants to wear it. Bodies can get blasted with crystal energy very easily, especially sensitive bodies.

In my experience, the safest crystals to have around are clear crystals. Clear crystals are like white light. Just like white light is safer to use than color rays, clear crystals are safer than colored ones. If you recall, white light is safe because it is the easiest for the body to absorb and assimilate. It is the main energetic fuel your body absorbs from the air and the earth, and it contains the full spectrum of light that your body can digest and use for whatever is required. In a similar way, clear crystals can provide a full spectrum of light energy that is naturally balanced and easy to assimilate.

I am fond of selenite because it is widely available, very gentle, and low-maintenance. It has a natural cleansing quality that I enjoy having around, but I don't use it much for healing. Clear quartz is my go-to for healing crystals. Quartz crystals need more cleaning than selenite, but they are better for using as healing tools because they don't dissolve or splinter like selenite and they are clearer conduits for projecting light through.

You don't need to have crystals of every color and kind. You don't need to spend a bunch of money on crystals. You don't need physical crystals at all, in fact. You can tap into their energy without having to possess them. If you are interested in working with them physically, I recommend getting one clear quartz wand or point and some clear quartz pebbles to experiment with.

The following list contains the most important qualities to keep in mind when selecting a crystal to use as a wand in healing.

- Clear quartz for safety of white light and practicality of multiple applications.
- A single point on one end and rounded or blunt on the other end for energy hygiene and safety.
- Cut to focus a laser-like beam of light out of the pointed end.
- Polished for ease of cleaning.
- The highest clarity you can find or afford.
- Make sure it feels easy to hold.

If you buy a cut and polished crystal wand, be sure to store and handle it carefully to avoid damage. They can be expensive, so you might like to experiment with something on the low end before investing in something you may not use much. Raw crystal points are affordable and work great, just don't leave them in a salt water bath. They don't like that. The salt will get into the tiny cracks and crevices and start eroding the integrity of the crystal.

You can use your wand as an extension of your hand during session work. You can use it to cut cords, clear energy, or energize. And just like your hands, it is important to keep it clean as you work.

If you are interested in working with crystal grids or layouts, you can get a handful of polished clear quartz pebbles. Yep. Simple pebbles like the ones you find in the dollar dish of your new age supply shop. Once you clear and charge them, they will be the perfect tools and you can afford to have enough for all the major energy centers or grid points you want to put a crystal on.

There are plenty of resources out there for crystal healing techniques, including crystal grids and layouts, so I'm not going to go into it here. I'm just offering a bit of basic information that you should know before going crazy with crystals. I know crystals are really popular and it is tempting to start collecting, but it really doesn't take much when it comes to crystals. In my experience, less is definitely more.

These days, I rarely use crystals. I do like making crystal essences to add to my smudge spray to super charge it. And I also like to use crystals when I am praying for someone. I will pull a card for that person and place a crystal on it and place that next to a candle. I will light the candle and pray for that person's healing. I imagine the card represents the person, the crystal is clearing energy for that person, and the candle flame is transmuting that energy. It's basically a simple crystal layout for remote healing. After the healing is complete, I clear the crystal and put it away.

Crystals require mindful care and respect. They require a bit less care than plants, but they do need to be cleaned regularly and stored in ways that won't negatively affect the energy of your space. I am a minimalist when it comes to crystals because I have worked with them a lot and I am very sensitive to their energy and what my body likes.

Here are some reasons why you might like to be a crystal minimalist, too:

- The more crystals, the more cleaning and care.
- Different kinds of crystals put out different kinds of energies which can be discordant.
- For an already highly-activated energy field, more activation is not helpful.
- The energy of neglected crystals can be unpleasant.
- Being conservative with crystal consumption is being mindful of sustainability and awareness that more crystals requires mining more minerals from the earth.

Now that we have some basic crystal knowledge, let's look at ways we can keep ourselves and our crystal friends happy.

## EXERCISE :: CLEAR + CHARGE A CRYSTAL

**1.** Pick any crystal you happen to have around. It could be a pebble, a point, or a piece of jewelry.
**2.** Invoke.
**3.** Scan the size of the field of the crystal to establish a baseline.
**4.** Scan to see how much energetic congestion is in the crystal.
**5.** Use the invocation to clear it: "It is my intent to clear any and all unhelpful, negative, or toxic energy stored in this crystal now."
**6.** Scan again to see if there is any left and repeat the clearing as needed.
**7.** Clear your hands.
**8.** Scan the size of the crystal's field after clearing the energy. Did it change?
**9.** Scan with the scale of "how much" to see how much programming/imprinting is in the crystal.
**10.** Use the invocation to clear them: "It is my intent to clear any and all programming and imprinting in this crystal and to also clear anything that doesn't allow that now."
**11.** Scan again to see if the programs/implants have cleared and repeat the clearing as needed.
**12.** Clear your hands.
**13.** Scan the field of the crystal to see if the size changed after clearing programs.
**14.** Once the crystal is clear of all unhelpful energies and programs, clear your hands in preparation for charging the crystal with fresh energy.
**15.** Using the energy projecting technique, project a beam of light into the crystal to charge it. Crystals can hold a lot of energy, so make sure you are consciously sourcing energy and not draining your body's personal energy as you pack it in.
**16.** Scan the field of the crystal again to see how big it is after charging it. You may need to start your scan from several feet away or more.

What did you find? Isn't it amazing how powerful the field of a cleared and charged crystal can be? Having crystals cleared and charged with positive energy also helps make their fields more comfortable to be in, especially if you are sensitive to crystal energy. Even so, it is also helpful to put crystals away when you're not using them.

## EXERCISE :: STORE YOUR CRYSTAL

**1.** Make sure your crystal is cleared and ready to be stored.
**2.** Scan the field of the crystal.
**3.** Instruct the crystal to turn off by pointing at it and saying, "Crystal, turn off" or by using the invocation, "It is my intent that this crystal turn off now."
**4.** Scan the field again. Did it get smaller?
**5.** Wrap the crystal in silk or leather.
**6.** Scan the field again. Did it get smaller?
**7.** Put the crystal away in a special place that is either not in your bedroom or if you don't have another room, as far from your bed as possible.
**8.** When it is time to use your crystal, reactivate it by telling it, "Crystal, turn on" or invoking for it to be turned on.

It is best to clear crystals before putting them away. There are many ways of clearing, charging, using, and storing crystals. These are a few simple ways to do it. You have your scanning tool that you can use in combination with any other practices to see what is most beneficial for you and the way you work.

The most important thing I can share about crystals is that they are conscious beings who deserve our care and respect, like plants and animals. Please be mindful of taking only what crystals you need. Be grateful for their gifts, and care for them as you would another being. If you feel that any of the crystal beings in your care are not being sufficiently cared for or honored, you can release them to another person who will use them mindfully or give them back to the earth with offerings of gratitude.

## SELF-CARE RITUALS

Any time we set an intention to heal, to clear, or to go deeper into our practices, we will receive whatever is required for that. This is helpful to remember as you continue with your practice of lightwork. The more you are interested in becoming free of limitations, the more will come up for clearing. It is infinitely helpful to recognize that every single upset that arises is a divine opportunity to release the blocks to love.

Dealing with all of our psychic trash can feel overwhelming sometimes, but thankfully we have mighty helpers. Keep handing all that heavy energy over to spirit and let yourself be lifted up. We are truly never doing this work alone.

I recommend setting yourself up with some structure for self-care so that it is automatic and you are continuously banking that energy. That way, you'll have a constant reserve, and in times of stress you can avoid getting totally frazzled, depleted, and feeling at your wit's end.

Remember, caring for yourself is the most important thing you can do for world health and healing. Only you can clear your own portion of the world's insanity. If you don't do your own inner work, all the outer work means nothing. It doesn't matter how much service you appear to be doing if you aren't caring for your primary responsibility: yourself.

Here are some self-care practices I recommend integrating into your routine so that they become part of your healthy lifestyle habits:

- Cut cords: very helpful to do each night before bed.
- Clearing: helpful to do mini clearings every day and a thorough one weekly.
- Grounding: very important to check in with grounding every day.
- Listening: notice any time something feels off and take appropriate steps.
- Take salt baths: good to do on a weekly basis.

One way I've found to stay in a high-vibe space to keep my energy clear and my body resilient is to layer mindfulness into my daily routines. If you build self-care rituals into existing routines, it will be easier to remember to do them. For example, when brushing your teeth, imagine a strong Earth channel giving your body strength and power. Giving thanks for food and water when eating and drinking is a classic. Remember, when establishing new habits and ways of being, it is more sustainable to add one at a time and build organically.

Be gentle and loving with yourself. You are a precious and essential part of the universe. As you care for yourself, you are creating a wellspring of love and light within you to lift you up in times of hardship and to light the way for others in times of darkness and despair. As *A Course In Miracles* says, "I bless the world because I bless myself."

## SALT BATHS

I've mentioned salt baths a few times, but haven't fully explained what the deal is with them, so let's get into it a bit.

Salt baths are an easy and effective way to clear energy in your field. Just like a salt water bowl, the water absorbs the congested energy and the salt dissolves it. Remember, sodium chloride salt is what has the cleansing power, so use land or sea salt for your energy hygiene baths.

Epsom salts are magnesium crystals and will not give you the cleansing effect of sodium crystals, but they're great for unwinding. Magnesium crystals work on the blue ray, which is relaxing, both for the mental and physical bodies. Sodium chloride, on the other hand, works on the green ray. If you are using salt in a bath to clear your energy, you can add magnesium to relax, but make sure you get sodium in there for its cleansing effects.

Here are some salt bath ingredients to play with:

- Cleansing: salt, lavender, tea tree, rosemary, eucalyptus
- Detoxifying: coffee grounds
- Relaxing: epsom salts
- Alkalizing: baking soda

- Emotional healing: rose petals or rose oil

Get creative. Feel free to mix it up, but keep it simple, sweetheart. As with many other kinds of recipes, if you add too many ingredients, you might end up with conflicting energies.

For an effective salt bath, you will want to use between one and two cups of salt, depending on how big your tub is. It should be very salty tasting. Soak in the bath, shifting to get all body parts in for some minutes. Stay in for a total of 15 to 20 minutes. Longer is not helpful. Ask your body when it feels complete and honor that. A rinse in fresh water is typically indicated, but not always. Again, scan or ask your body if unsure.

With some healing modalities, salt baths are highly recommended after session work. For example, with Reiki all the focus is on energizing and that energy goes to work clearing things, but it can also easily trigger a healing reaction or crisis when symptoms temporarily worsen. Taking a salt bath after a Reiki session will help clear the energy that is releasing and lessen the symptoms. This works not just with Reiki, but with any modality that focuses on energizing.

Because Lightworker Training focuses on clearing first and energy is only added when and where needed, taking a salt bath after receiving session work is usually not helpful. You could be washing away the helpful energy that is maybe sealing leaks or doing other repair and balancing work. For Lightworker Training session work, it is more helpful for the recipient to take a salt bath *before* the session.

If you are unsure which category a modality falls into, either salt bath before or salt bath after, you can use the scanning technique. Using the scale of "how much," scan for "how much benefit will I receive from a salt bath be before this session?" and "how much benefit from a salt bath after?"

If you are a practitioner, caregiver, social worker, or service industry professional, I recommend taking regular salt baths once a week and again whenever you have an especially challenging day. If you have a big event interacting with a lot of people or traveling through airports, grounding and taking a salt bath afterward can be a game-changer. You might be surprised at how much energy can shift with a simple bath.

## ASCENSION PROCESS + DETOX SYMPTOMS

As mentioned in **Chapter 8: Chakra Form + Function + Clearing**, we are living in a time of great change. The process of raising our vibration and expanding our fields is known as ascension. Earth is going through changes and so are our bodies, which are extensions of the Earth.

The ascension process can feel very intense as whole systems are shifting in the planetary energy field and in our personal energy fields. Part of caring for ourselves and having compassion lies in the recognition that there is massive change unfolding. Understanding that ascension can trigger life-times of psychic baggage coming up for healing and uncomfortable physical detox symptoms in the body will help us stay more grounded as the process unfolds.

During a wave of ascension energy moving through the collective, you may experience or witness  a variety of detox symptoms. The following list includes the most common ones.

- Insomnia, restlessness
- Exhaustion, fatigue, overwhelm
- Depression, anxiety
- Body twitches and itches
- Tinnitus, dizziness, vertigo
- Headaches, blurred vision, brain fog
- Skin rashes, acne, eczema
- Allergies
- Flu-like symptoms
- Nausea, diarrhea
- Feeling emotional

These symptoms could be related to conditions other than ascension energy, so it is important to check in with your body. Ask if the symptom is ascension-related. Sometimes when we are experiencing symptoms we immediately jump to the conclusion that there is something wrong with us, but what if there was something right about it?

During big waves of ascension, our bodies are processing a lot. It can feel like living in a house that is being remodeled. Our nervous systems feel overloaded with all the energy coming through and it's important that we continue to ground and clear. It's also important to give the body whatever it requires without judgment. These little animal bodies are always doing their best and they can do so more easily without having to take on the additional burden of our resistance to what is happening.

Here are some vital practices for navigating huge energy shifts with more grace:

• Get your greens: dark green veggies, green juice, supplements.
• Plenty of fresh food: avoid all processed food, eat mostly fruits and veggies.
• Re-mineralize: give your body extra minerals and electrolytes.
• Hydrate: get used to drinking more water on a regular basis.
• Exercise: walk, dance, stretch, bike, move your body every day.
• Salt baths: clear your energy field with a salt bath.
• Energy work: clear anything that is coming up for release.
• Ground: release all overwhelming energy into the Earth.
• Rest: arrange your schedule to get more quality rest and sleep.
• Unplug: put down the phone and get screen-free time.

## CONTINUING DISCERNMENT

As you continue with your exploration of lightwork, or anything else for that matter, be sure to use your intuitive tools to discern what is helpful for you. If you weren't sensitive, compassionate, and somewhat enlightened, you most likely would not be reading this.

You have what it takes to know what is right for you in the moment. It doesn't matter if someone else got great results from this, that, or the other thing. The question to ask is, "Is this helpful for me right now?"

Whether it's a class, a book, a practice, a dietary change, or any other kind of tool, if you are looking at some choices and you'd like to get more information, rather than trying to figure it out, I recommend asking a question and allowing yourself to receive the answer. The answer may come as a feeling, a picture, a knowingness, a sensation in your body, or a voice in your mind.

If you don't seem to get an answer or would like more information, you can scan the energy or ask your body. You can also just be with the energy of the question and see what pops up in your field. Maybe the answer will come through a synchronous occurrence, something that catches your attention, or something someone says to you.

The universe works in mysterious ways and it answers your every question. Your job is to learn how to tune in, ask helpful questions, and listen for the answer.

Nobody has your highest and best interests in mind like your very own higher self, so get to know it and trust it.

## IT GETS BETTER

No doubt if you are reading this book and you've gotten this far, you are seriously committed to your healing, your spiritual growth, and your wellness. Perhaps, like me, you have done a lot of personal inquiry, study, and practice on the road to recovering your health and sanity. Perhaps, like me, you sometimes doubt if it's possible for you to overcome your trauma and feelings of brokenness.

Please know this: it does get better. If you keep going, if you keep committing to loving yourself free, you will find more peace, resiliency, and even joy. That's not to say things will stop being intense. These are intense times. We live in an age of extremes. We are being pushed to evolve and indeed we are evolving, even if it seems like some people are being dragged kicking and screaming into the next level of awareness.

The tools I've presented here can assist you on your healing journey, but you don't need them. You can make up your own. The important thing is to keep showing up in willingness to do whatever it takes to liberate yourself from the unloving and limiting beliefs of your social conditioning. Whatever path you choose, if your intention is clear, you will reach your target.

It amazes me that I've been able to get as free as I have in the last ten or so years. I really believed that I would be bound to the limitations of my past trauma for the rest of my life. The following story illustrates a possibility of something else.

As a kid, I was dissociated from my body. As a teen and young adult, I would let people do whatever they wanted to my body because I wanted them to like me. As a beginning yoga practitioner in my early twenties, I couldn't really connect to my body or my breath. For most of my life I couldn't really connect with my body unless I was getting high, having sex, or in physical pain. From my infancy until my late thirties, I spent a lot of time getting very sick or very hurt.

When I started doing energy healing work in my thirties, I felt like a fraud. I still felt so broken. Even though I had a miraculous experience of myself as light when I was in the hospital, I was skeptical of my ability to fully reconnect with that state of being. Nevertheless, I kept doing the work. I was starting to feel the power of the energy working through me and that was exciting.

The practice of mindfulness and sensing subtle energy helped me to feel embodied for the first time in my life. I tuned in and noticed more. I quieted my mind and listened. The more I focused on being present and open to receiving feelings, impressions, and sensations, the more I experienced them. The more I asked my body about things, the more easily I could discern what it shared with me, and the stronger our connection became.

Now not only am I able to connect with and feel my body, but through it I can tap into the oneness of nature. I can tune in and feel organic reality wherever I am. I don't have to go anywhere to be in nature, because I am always in nature. Truth is, I always have been, but I didn't know because I couldn't feel it. Now I can.

I can feel my body's connection to the Earth. I can feel the plants, animals, and minerals. I can feel their vibrations in my body. I can set an intention like, "I wonder what those plants feel like?" and in a flash, I'm there, in the field of their consciousness. I can see their rays of light and hear the tones of their frequencies like a chorus, all chiming together. I can feel the sway of their spiraling dance moving my body.

The connection is psychedelic. It's ecstatic. It's even orgasmic. And it's weirdly not a big deal. It's extremely comforting, and it might actually be my true state of being: giggling, crying, feeling waves of bliss and grief wash over me, talking to hummingbirds, whispering to flowers, and listening deeply to everything singing the song of creation.

It's possible that it's your natural state of being, too.

## CHAPTER 11 :: KEY POINTS

- In the oneness lies all power, safety, and knowledge.
- You are not your addictions, your trauma, or your pain.
- Your human experience can never diminish the light of your spirit, even if you can't see the light.
- Crystals and plants have consciousness just like everything else in the universe.
- Self care is mandatory for longevity and resiliency.
- Only you know what your boundaries are at any given moment.
- Practice discernment to honor what is true for you.
- Keep being curious and asking questions to receive more information.
- Everything is an experiment.
- Everything is for your learning.
- Ecstatic connection with the oneness is possible.

## CHAPTER 11 :: INTEGRATION TIPS

• If you're feeling exhausted/sick/frazzled, ask your body: Is it ascension symptoms? Is it even yours?

• Sort energy every evening: return to sender anything in your field that is not yours; reclaim any energy/power that is yours that you left with someone or somewhere else.

• Notice your personal energy cycles and start to plan accordingly. Give yourself more time to rest when you have less energy, plan activities at times when you have more energy, and build recovery time into your schedule.

• Integrate one habit at a time, one step at a time. Slow, steady, organic growth is key. Nature didn't get it wrong.

## CHAPTER 11 :: PRACTICUM POSSIBILITIES

**Reflect on Your Journey:** (about 15 minutes)

Take a moment to write in your journal about your experience in this course. Here are some questions to consider: What were the most valuable tools you learned? What did you like? What did you not like? Has your energy, awareness, or experience of life shifted in any way?

Once you have reflected, look back at what you wrote as your original intention for doing this work. Notice how you feel now. What is your intention moving forward?

**Client Lightwork Session Practice:** (up to an hour)

Invite a friend to receive session work from you. You may choose to work in-person or remotely. Perform a complete lightwork session with your friend. Receive feedback and share your experiences.

**Graduation Ceremony:** (as long as you like)

Take some time and space to honor your journey through this course. Here are some elements that you can mix and match to create a ceremony for yourself:

• Go to a place that feels powerful to you: the forest, the beach, the desert, the mountains, either in your body or in your mind.
• Spend some time meditating: go on a journey, commune with the Earth.
• Ask spirit for a symbol of graduating to the next level of your work. See what shows up.
• Put on some music and dance, sing/play a song, make some art/an installation/an altar.
• Go for a soak or swim.
• Make a special meal or treat.
• Share your accomplishment with a friend who loves to celebrate you.
• Get a tattoo.
• Take the day off.
• Give yourself an award.

# CHAPTER 12:
# REPRISE

**Remember this**


You are a spark of creation, each moment a new
beginning containing infinite choice
a sovereign creator whose natural state
is miraculous peace, freedom, and grace

You are strength of stillness, the patience of stones
what is healing is knowing you're already whole
lifetimes of trauma dissolve to the cause
in the power and presence of love that you are

You are quickness of mind, shape-shift like lightning
and every thought you describe spells an outcome
the split in your mind never really occurred
all choices in time lead back to the beloved

You are currents of knowing that flow back to source

the more you will listen, the more you will trust
that denial could only be useful for lies
is the truth of the teaching that sings in your heart

You are pure innocence, eternally beaming
co-creating with source intelligence streaming
through the infinite mind wherein all things are known
and remembrance that you were never alone

You are the master of forms, cultivating perfection
releasing all judgment you find liberation
from struggle and energy drains of attachment
to the harvested jewels of love without limit

You are beauty of balance and sovereign relation
reflecting abundant spheres of creation
spiraling energy moves all throughout you
the love that you be is within and without you

You are deepest mystery, ever unfolding
fields within fields, expanding, collapsing
you are the cycle of forms ever-changing
and the still point between the inhale and exhale

You are aim of intention and radiant wisdom
channeling infinite source information
you teach what you most need to learn on your journey
with no time or distance outside love's expansion

You are the pinnacle of every achievement
sure-footed, you rise on the path of ascension
boundaries of structure are no limitation
just a focus of time spent in this incarnation

You are limitless space that connects constellations
an inventor exploring the mind of creation
your vision inspires your own evolution

and the world's wake up call to love's revolution

You are love of all things, merged in the oneness
ecstatic communion with all of life's sources
feel into the truth of your daydreams and see
heaven on earth is here now if you'll be it

# APPENDIX 1:
# LIGHTWORK SESSION PROTOCOL

**1. INVOCATION**

**2. CORD CUTTING:**
    **A. GENERAL: BIOFIELD**
    **B. LOCAL: CHAKRAS/SPECIFIC AREAS**

**3. CLEARING:**
    **A. GENERAL: BIOFIELD + RAYS OF LIGHT**
    **B. LOCAL:**
        **1. CHANNELS**
        **2. CHAKRAS**
        **3. TISSUES/PHYSICAL BODY**

**4. ENERGIZING:**
    **A. DEPLETED CHAKRAS/FIELDS/CHANNELS**
        **1. SEAL LEAKS**
    **B. HARMONIZING:**
        **1. CHAKRAS/FIELDS/CHANNELS**
            **A. SCAN ACTIVITY LEVEL**
            **B. ACTIVATE OR INHIBIT AS REQUIRED**

**5. SHIELDING:**
    **A. INSTALL & PROGRAM:**
        **1. CHAKRA SHIELDS**
        **2. BIOFIELD SHIELD**

**6. SEAL THE PROCESS:**
    **A. INVOKE FOR COMPLETION**
    **B. GIVE THANKS**
    **C. CUT CORDS**
    **D. CLEAR YOURSELF + SPACE**

# APPENDIX 2:
# CHAKRA CHART

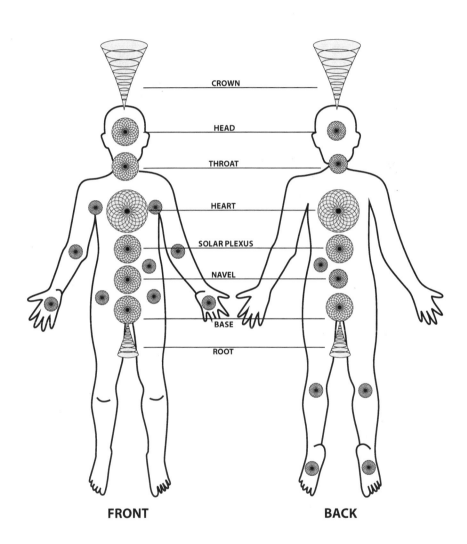

CROWN

HEAD

THROAT

HEART

SOLAR PLEXUS

NAVEL

BASE

ROOT

**FRONT**

**BACK**

# ACKNOWLEDGMENTS

Infinite love and gratitude to my writing coach, editor, mentor, and muse, the multi-talented Nick Jaina. Your support and guidance were absolutely essential to the creation of this book and it's no exaggeration to say that it would be lllppmmoo without you.

I am grateful for the immensely helpful feedback and edit suggestions from Alisha Westerman. Listening to your notes got me through the second round edits when I was exhausted. Thank you!

I give thanks and acknowledgment to Master Choa Kok Sui and Teresa Evans. Pranic Healing was the foundation of my lightwork practice and many tools in this book come straight from Master Choa's teachings which I received from my teacher, Teresa. Thank you, Teresa, for all the hours you spent mentoring me and all your generosity.

I am thankful for the teachings in *A Course in Miracles* and Reverend Jennifer Hadley. *ACIM* is the backbone of my mindset awareness and teachings. Thank you, Jennifer, for bringing me back to the well and making the teachings so accessible and practical.

I am grateful for the teachings of *Access Consciousness* and Jeneth Blackert. Access has given me the tools of asking questions, talking to entities, and opening to more possibility. Thank you, Jeneth, for introducing me to the weird and wonderful world of *Access*.

I acknowledge the Chinook tribes and all native peoples of the land I inhabit. I humbly ask forgiveness for being an uninvited guest here. I ask forgiveness on behalf of my ancestors. I am deeply indebted to you and this sacred land. I will do better. I offer my loving respect and gratitude.

I give thanks to the nature spirits of the land and all the mineral, plant, and animal beings that bless this place with their presence and their medicine. Thank you for reminding me always of the truth and for singing the songs of creation.

I acknowledge the tree beings and the nonconsensual way in which your bodies were taken to make the paper for this book. Please forgive us. I love you. I am so grateful for you and I will do my best to give back.

Thank you to the students of Lightworker Training who requested this book and all the clients, students, circles, and communities I have had the opportunity to serve and learn from.

I am supremely grateful for the illness that introduced me to the Masters of my lineage and the light of my being. Thank you for waking me up.

And I am, as always, in awe beyond expression for the great mystery of universal consciousness that flows through all things. Thank you for the gift of life and all the moments of grace experienced in the oneness.

May we all be blessed with knowing how beloved we are and feeling gratitude for all that has been given us.

So be it.

# INDEX